Inspiring Women

Living an Unstoppable Life with Purpose, Power, and Passion

Marie Fratoni

Published by
Hybrid Global Publishing
333 E 14th Street
#3C
New York, NY 10003

Manufactured in the United States of America, or in the United Kingdom when distributed elsewhere.

Fratoni, Marie
Inspiring Women: Living an Unstoppable Life with Purpose, Power, and Passion
    ISBN: 978-1-961757-62-2
    eBook: 978-1-961757-63-9
    LCCN: 2024945706

Cover design by: Natasha Clawson
Copyediting by: Claudia Volkman
Interior design by: Suba Murugan
Author photo by: Kris Janovitz

CONTENTS

Contents

INTRODUCTION

Marie Fratoni

Women are inspiring, and I am lucky enough to be surrounded by women who daily display courage, intelligence, compassion, and service to clients, family, and members of their community. And you are lucky, too, for they are vividly active in your lives as well. They are business owners, consultants, moms, and aunties—and they sometimes take on the heralded role of "fairy godmother" to those that are in need.

This book was called forth by readers of the first volume of *Inspiring Women*. In fact, several people enthusiastically encouraged me to produce a second book and basically invited themselves to be considered as one of the new book's collaborative authors. The call was answered, and this latest edition of *Inspiring Women* is here. In this version, being unstoppable became a theme woven throughout many of the stories. These women don't let obstacles stop them. Instead, they find creative solutions to handle tough situations.

Women are the gifts that keep on giving. Despite life's twists and turns, women dig in their "high heels" and tough it out. They keep moving forward amid the myriads of circumstances that need to be dealt with each day. They have learned to push forward to reach goals, accomplish great achievements, and pull from all aspects of physical, emotional, spiritual, financial, and social constraints. Some have pivoted, changed careers, gotten new positions, and acted responsibly to take care of themselves and others. They didn't give up. They simply changed course. In fact, I think you would agree that women have multiple interests and passions and are so very talented. Sometimes it is difficult to narrow down our skill sets into one satisfying business or profession. Some become serial entrepreneurs with multiple streams of income. Why not?

Women have made significant contributions to various fields such as business, science, art, politics, education, and social justice. Recognizing their achievements highlights their impact and the difference they make, and it encourages continued progress. Inspiring women serve as role models, especially for young girls and women. Spotlighting successful women can inspire others to pursue their dreams and overcome their challenges.

This book is designed to touch you so you can see yourself in the stories of these talented authors. You can be inspired, have a giggle, borrow a tip or two, and realize that there is always something around the corner in life and business. We want you to be ready with drive and the right resources to make your move.

Inspiring women serve as role models, especially for young girls, college students, and women who would like to venture into business or entrepreneurism. Seeing the stories of successful women can inspire other women to pursue their dreams and overcome life's obstacles. Today, more than ever, we need women to lead. We need women who are willing to generously share their breakdowns and triumphs, their stories of courage, grit, and resilience.

The contributions of many women have been overlooked or underrepresented in history. Recognizing inspiring women helps to correct historical narratives and ensures a more accurate and inclusive representation of history, or "herstory." Women don't need to be on the Forbes Billionaire List to be powerful and successful. Some live simply, do their work quietly, and serve their clients and community with excellence. Books like this one showcase everyday women pursuing a passion, sharing their expertise with others, and plowing through some very tough times. Acknowledging their unique perspectives, approaches, and contributions to various fields enriches our understanding and fosters innovation and creativity. The authors of this book represent many diverse businesses and professional tracks. Each one has taken on this book project to look inside themselves, consider their readers, and write a chapter that is juicy to read, highlighting something they overcame, sharing what they created, and leaving the reader with a simple lesson of hope and a "you can do it, too" message.

Women in business serve as role models and mentors for other women, inspiring them to pursue leadership positions and career advancement. This helps close the gender gap in leadership and create a more equitable workplace and business environment. I hope that the messages in this book inspire you to take a course, go back to school, hire a coach, secure a mentor, and take positive action toward living your best life. All we have is NOW.

Let's celebrate these inspiring women who are living a life of unstoppable purpose and passion. I invite you to hitch yourself to their stories and see yourself soar.

LIVING YOUR LIFE PURPOSE LEADS TO AN AMAZING LIFE!

Marie Fratoni

In 1987 I trusted my strong intuition and hired my first life coach. I thought that working with her would make my life, business, and relationships better; therefore, I would be happier. It worked! It was a genius move on my part and an investment that continues to pay off to this day.

So many "pooh-pooh" the idea of creating a life purpose statement. But I wonder how many of those who have this opinion and bias simply made up something that sounded good in the moment, resonated with them quickly, and then thought they would easily have a life that worked and was fulfilling, simply because they said, "My purpose is to teach," or "My purpose is to honor animals," or something similar. Or maybe they thought that a life purpose was something they merely liked to do and would make for a great business. I beg to differ! However, I acknowledge that this is a good place to start when creating a life that works, a life you love.

I would love to share my life purpose statement with you. I created this overall life-affirming statement in 1987, and I continue to use it today as a guiding force—my true north—when choosing what will bring me joy, ease, and fulfillment. Here it is:

My purpose is to dynamically express myself through adventuresome social camaraderie in ways that make a difference to myself and others.

These are not merely words that when strung together sound good. Rather, they are specifically crafted and selected from stories, situations, events, jobs, and occasions throughout my life, beginning with my very first year. Designing this statement was a process, led by a certified coach, and recorded, and it covers the span of my life up until the present moment.

After a time of discussion, wordsmithing, and creatively crafting and speaking it aloud, a dynamic sentence begins to emerge. Joy is present when it is spoken. The heart smiles as it is whispered. And then a practice of mirrorwork begins, where speaking this statement over and over begins to land inside of our body, soul, and spirit. A feeling of well-being arises. When I worked with my coach, she listened intently to see if it matched the intended hallmarks and then helped to ground it inside of me using a simple neuro-linguistic anchoring exercise. It seemed like magic, yet some work and attention were required to achieve this outcome.

This is an eye-opening process and gives us a glimpse of how our personalities have developed over the course of our lifetime. Once these synergistic events have been documented, we then begin to notice similar themes. We note our feelings and body sensations as we uncover what it's like when life seems easy, we are happy, and things seem to flow effortlessly. We become aware of how that positively impacts and imprints into our bodies, our tissues, and our emotional selves.

When we are not living on purpose, it seems like the adage "pushing a square peg into a round hole." It's not fun—it's exhausting. In the 1980s, I was invited to be a corporate training instructor for an international consulting firm. On the surface it sounded like it would be a fantastic opportunity. I was invited because of my outgoing personality, experience with corporate training, and of course, all my professional connections. I would be traveling three weeks out of each month, but I would be compensated well, my travel expenses would be covered, and I would forge ahead in my career. It seemed to be a good fit.

Unfortunately, this gig was short-lived. I had to mold myself into someone I truly wasn't. For someone who excelled in interpersonal training skills, I struggled with this opportunity being information-based, didactic, and heavy on delivering very specific, very technical content during the four-day trainings. I had to dig deep, memorize the material—in short, it was one of the hardest jobs I've ever had. It also was political, and I was the new kid. I was not able to freely and dynamically express myself. We all were monitored tightly, and I felt like I couldn't breathe. The travel was fun, the clients were delightful, but my full self-expression was constrained. And yet I still lasted for two years. I was happy outside of the office, but even now, just remembering those days makes me feel majorly icky.

Creating and living your life purpose profoundly impacts your life in numerous positive ways. Defining and pursuing your life purpose will lead to an amazing life, especially when used as a vector that has direction and force. Before big life endeavors, considering work ventures, joining programs, or pursuing a passion, I always run things by my life purpose.

- Does it resonate?
- Does it have the component of "adventuresome social camaraderie"?
- Will I be able to dynamically express myself?
- Will it make a difference, not just for me, but for others, too?

If the answers to these questions are "yes," then there is a high likelihood that it will work out. If not, then, tempting as it is, I will move away. In some instances, I will see what I can do to make it fit and work. Yes, I still do this today, and I trust the process. It works.

Having a defined life purpose gives a clear direction that helps you set meaningful goals—and achieve them. You'll be able to prioritize actions and decisions that are aligned with your purpose. Armed with a focused sense of purpose, you are more likely to invest your time and energy in the right types of activities and communities that are productive and fulfilling. In fact, you will know quickly whether the opportunity will work for you or not. When you are not "on purpose," stress, pain, upset, delays, problems, and seemingly unworkable situations start to rear their head. These are clues that something is off and needs to be readjusted.

Discovering and knowing your life purpose can trickle down to your lifetime vision, your mission, your values, and your intended results. There is an easy flow, and when explored and planned, higher levels of well-being are present, because you did the big, important work in the beginning.

Purpose-driven individuals often report higher levels of happiness and life satisfaction, as they are engaged in pursuits that resonate with their core values and passions. They feel that their efforts are meaningful, consciously intended, and impactful. A strong sense of purpose acts as a powerful motivator. Maybe it's too much to suggest that when your future endeavors are filtered through your life purpose statement, they will work out without a hitch. We still need to do the planning, conducting the activities to get the work done, often while adjusting course. But we start out with a high probability of success.

Living with purpose attracts like-minded people who share similar values and goals. This can lead to deeper, more meaningful connections and a supportive community and staff. A sense of purpose can foster empathy and compassion toward others, which in turn will create a positive impact on you and those around you. A purposeful life encourages continuous personal growth, so you are likely to seek out new experiences, learn new skills, and develop new talents. This results in a boost of self-esteem and confidence and reinforces your beliefs in your judgment and abilities. I firmly believe that living your life's purpose will result in better mental health, too, reducing the risk of depression, anxiety, and negative stressors. You may even gain better physical health. The icing on the cake is that living your life with purpose allows you to contribute something greater than yourself, thus leaving a positive legacy and contribution that will affect your life, the lives of those you touch, and those whose lives they touch.

It is well worth doing the work to get to your own divine life purpose statement. Allow me to share a few examples of what I have created from being aligned with my life purpose:

- Becoming a transformational business coach and creating group programs that include fun, camaraderie, making a difference, and developing new clients
- Offering retreats for business development, transformation, relaxation, and fun, led in the United States and Italy
- Serving women business owners for the past fifteen years through a professional development network I created
- Leading masterminds
- Being a compilation book author and host

Doing the work of creating my life purpose statement was so beneficial to me that I became certified in conducting and leading this process for more than one hundred of my clients. This tool is invaluable, and I am forever grateful for its guiding presence in my life. I now live a life that is true to my authentic self, where every bold action and any big decisions are chosen with purpose, presence, and power.

Marie Fratoni is a sought-after business coach, professional speaker, and transformational retreat leader. She is a champion of women! Marie's programs provide professionals with relevant content, revenue-generating strategies, and uplifting events that boost confidence and business savvy. She loves helping her clients double or triple their income. Marie is the CEO of Get Clients Everywhere and the founder and leader of the Women's Professional Development Network (WPDN), a thirteen-year-old international community of women entrepreneurs. She also leads popular annual retreats in Italy for busy professionals who want a magical getaway to rest, relax, and rejuvenate. Marie lives in the Atlanta area and works globally helping women entrepreneurs connect and prosper.

getclientseverywhere.com

RESILIENCE—THE CATALYST THAT MAKES EVERYTHING ELSE POSSIBLE

Alison Chandler

I pulled a card and asked my family members seated around the table, "What's my favorite thing about me?"

Without hesitation, my daughter, Lucy, proudly chimed in, "Me." Wow—what an insightful little girl. She is my miracle after years of struggling with infertility. Having her is a dream come true!

My husband, Jonathan, said, "Creativity." Looks like he knows me pretty well, too. We're playing the card game Betcha Don't Know, taking turns asking questions to see how well we know each another.

Creativity has always been present in my life. I enjoy getting lost in it, and it helps me see possibilities and solve problems, which is crucial in my personal and professional life.

My mom adds, "It's your positive attitude." Spot on! Positivity is a big part of who I am. Have you ever had something so natural you didn't even realize it was a defining part of you until someone else pointed it out? For me, it's optimism. I tend to find the bright side in most situations, and looking back, it's helped me bounce back more times than I realize.

But then I surprised myself by blurting out, "Resilience."

At first I thought, *What a boring word*. But the more I thought about it, the more I realized how true it is. Without resilience, I might not be here. I wouldn't have overcome the challenges of infertility, expressed my creativity, and maintained my positivity. Resilience is the foundation that makes everything else possible.

Without resilience, I might be telling you a different story. I could have developed a fear of taking risks and missed out on sky diving, scuba diving, becoming an entrepreneur, learning more about who I was, and so much more.

Realizing Narcolepsy

You wouldn't think resilience and naps go hand in hand, but for me, they do. My family used to joke about how I could shamelessly sleep anytime, anywhere. On boat rides, at concerts, and even during massive hurricanes.

Anytime I drove for longer than four hours, I pulled over in a restaurant parking lot or state welcome center to catch a few Z's. Now, that might sound risky, but I always traveled with my trusty sidekick—Casey, a Yorkie who thought she was a guard dog. I felt safe knowing her ferocious bark would wake me up.

In graduate school, my now husband and I had a long-distance relationship, and our visits always included naps. And when we rented our first house together in New Orleans, we didn't celebrate with a fancy dinner or hitting the town. Oh no, we celebrated by taking a lovely nap on the cozy carpet in the walk-in closet.

Have you ever noticed that one of your habits isn't as common as you thought? Well, that's what happened when we discovered our napping habit wasn't just a little offbeat—there was a reason behind it. We found out that we both have sleep apnea and joked that our wedding cake would have a couple wearing CPAP masks.

The sleep apnea diagnosis and treatment helped me for a while—until it didn't. I went back to taking naps at the end of the day and waking up for a couple of hours before bedtime. But it was never hard to go back to sleep. Yet no matter how long I slept, I never felt rested.

We later moved to Atlanta, and one day while I was shopping with my mom, we stopped at Starbucks. After drinking one of their larger coffees, I felt something I hadn't felt in a very long time—I was wide awake, as if a switch had just been flipped! What happened to my lifeforce? Am I sleeping my life away? It was like waking up to the reality that I had been living a subdued life.

I knew I had to dig deeper and uncover the root cause of this relentless fatigue. Even though adding doctor visits and countless tests to the days I was already struggling to get through wasn't easy, it was necessary to reclaim my life. Eventually, after being misdiagnosed with other conditions, I was finally diagnosed with narcolepsy.

The diagnosis wasn't the immediate relief I had hoped for. Initially, it brought denial, frustration, and even anger. But over time, my natural optimism kicked in, and I began to see the bright side. I finally understood why getting eight hours of shut-eye felt like a blink. I was relieved to know it wasn't about being lazy or unmotivated. It taught me a valuable lesson to be mindful of my energy and set healthy boundaries. I was ready to approach life with a fresh perspective and a renewed sense of purpose.

By tapping into my inner resilience and creativity, I found greater clarity, confidence, and fulfillment in all areas of my life. This journey helped me reconnect to my soul essence, and emerge with a deeper understanding of who I am and what truly lights me up.

Connecting the Dots

Living with narcolepsy is like living with an invisible party crasher. It shows up uninvited at the worst possible times, casting a shadow on what matters most. Canceling plans at the last minute, even when you've been counting down the days. Wanting to engage in great conversations but too drained to speak.

To this day, I wonder what happened to the daring girl I used to be. As a child, I was known for my vibrant spirit, creativity, confidence, and compassion. I always embraced new experiences fearlessly. More than a little mischievous and with a hint of stubbornness, my father claimed that I was allergic to the word "no."

Even though it's never been confirmed, I believe that an accident I had when I was a child left me with more than scars. On Thanksgiving Day 1986, instead of enjoying our traditional family meal, I was rushed via Medivac to the Children's Hospital in Birmingham, Alabama, 150 miles away. I wasn't supposed to ride my bike, but that didn't stop me. I was gliding down the hill near our house, with enough momentum to take me all the way home. However, as I sped through the stop sign as I had done countless times before, I got hit by a car.

I have no memory of the accident, the helicopter ride, or time in the intensive care unit. Later, I learned I had a massive concussion and nine broken bones that required many years of reconstructive surgeries. To me, the whole experience felt normal. My friends still visited me, I got to eat as much mac and cheese as I wanted, and I could color all day long. And the minute I could, I hopped back on my bike and continued doing the things I loved.

Looking back, I now realize that my resilience and positive attitude carried me through without making it a big deal. It took more than twenty years to learn that the traumatic brain injury from that accident likely led to this lifelong condition, caused by the brain not producing the chemical responsible for deep, restorative sleep.

From Resilience to Passionate Purpose

I've become increasingly aware of the judgments from those who don't know or understand invisible conditions.

In my work emails, I frequently come across subject lines featuring phrases like "lack of motivation," "procrastination," or "lazy," implying a lack of drive or discipline. I find these quite frustrating and dismissive. I've also been told, "It must be nice to have the luxury of taking a nap," as if it's a choice rather than a necessity. I would much rather be active and engaged on the days I struggle to stay awake.

But despite the occasional naps and misunderstandings, I've found ways to accept this new reality with a positive attitude. Sometimes I feel fulfilled, that I'm living a full and vibrant life; other times, not so much. On those days I give myself the grace I would give to a friend.

I've learned to let go of others' expectations of what it means to be a working mom and a loving wife, and most of the time, I don't feel the need to explain myself. I incorporate resilience into my daily routine with adaptability, humor, and a positive mindset. I've redefined success on my terms.

My passion to make a difference and live my purpose inspires me to overcome the struggles and stay aligned with what truly matters. Without resilience, narcolepsy could be a good excuse to not participate in life, a reason to hold back from living fully and with intention.

Resilience has become my superpower, the catalyst that makes all things possible. It's guided me through life's challenges and frustrations with unwavering strength and determination. By tapping into my inner magic—my unique blend of resilience, creativity, and positivity—I've experienced profound clarity, renewed confidence, and a deep sense of joy. This has illuminated my purpose and fueled my passion to help others, ultimately making a positive impact on their lives and in the world.

Today, I've applied that resilience to my business, helping ambitious, heart-centered entrepreneurs to embrace their own unique gifts and talents to overcome obstacles with confidence. I empower them to transform their brands to reflect their true essence, unlocking their potential to shine brightly in the world and expand their impact. My experience has taught me that resilience isn't just about bouncing back—it's about thriving, growing, and inspiring others to do the same.

How will you let your resilience guide your journey and illuminate new possibilities?

Alison Chandler, an award-winning brand strategist, graphic designer, and speaker with more than twenty years of experience, holds an MFA from the Savannah College of Art and Design. She's dedicated to empowering ambitious, heart-centered clients with authority-building strategies and soulful messaging that deeply connect with dream clients. Her mission is to guide business owners to reclaim their unique strengths, step into their power, and fall in love with their businesses all over again—creating a massive impact.

alisonchandler.net

A FUNNY THING HAPPENED ON MY JOURNEY TO SELF-DISCOVERY

Sherri Danzig

For as long as I can remember, I've believed that I control what I manifest in my life. I get to choose; I can attract all I desire. So, it's incredibly frustrating to struggle with the one thing that has eluded me for years, the last thing that keeps me from feeling like I have it all. Grappling with this has made me question: Either my belief about manifestation is a bunch of hooey, or I'm a lousy manifester. But neither is true. I have a proven record of being a masterful manifester in many areas of my life—just not this one.

For the majority of my life, I have struggled with my weight. But knowing the steps to change my body has only added to my frustration. Apparently, knowing what you need to do and actually doing it are not the same thing. Who knew? No magic wand was going to work. It's not that easy, and it's not that quick. Damn it again.

The key to manifesting what I want so dearly is the same for anyone ready to leap over their giant roadblock of an unfulfilled and unsatisfied life. To be on the path of "I nailed it . . . I am living my best life" is really simple. You must change the story you've been telling yourself about your current situation.

You may be thinking, *Surely it can't only be changing the story you tell about yourself in order to change your entire life.* And yet your story, your belief of who you are, dictates everything. As Henry Ford said, "Whether you think you can, or you think you can't—you're right."

That one big thing that has eluded me all these years is my relationship with food. You see, I am an emotional eater. For me, food has been my favorite reward and my supreme nurturer. My story has been: No matter what happens to me, I can eat something yummy, and I won't feel as bad.

This story stems from my identity—in other words, how I think of myself. This includes what I believe I'm good at and what I believe I'm not. If you're like me, many of these stories have been passed down from our families for generations. For example, I learned at a very early age that "the women in my family don't have flat stomachs," so I believed I could never have one. We're all taught these narratives as if they're fact. You might think of yourself as smart or a poor student, the "life of the party" or a wallflower, naturally athletic or uncoordinated and clumsy.

Until you identify how you see yourself, you cannot distinguish between what is true and what is merely family folklore or a personal anecdote created from past experiences. These stories are often steeped in fear. Only through self-reflection can we discover which stories are actually holding us back. And with this acknowledgment, we can rewrite our stories, letting go of the past and creating new narratives for our lives.

I decided to embark on a journey of self-discovery with my usual "all in" approach so I could understand the story that has kept me, well, *fat*. I don't love the word or the identity it brings, preferring to think of myself as *chubby*, but I've been in denial. And honestly, the medical term for someone carrying as much extra weight as I do is *clinically obese*.

Ironically, my story of being a food addict begins with growing up in a restaurant. The year I started sixth grade, my parents opened a delicatessen, and as the only daughter, I was expected to help out. It became my weekend and summer job, and even when I went to college, my friends knew they could find me at the deli during winter holidays, elbow-deep in a bowl of potato salad.

This experience gave me ease and confidence in the kitchen. You can task me with providing dinner for fifty, and I'm excitedly rolling up my sleeves, planning the menu, shopping, and cooking a delicious gourmet meal. This identity has enriched my life by becoming one of my favorite ways to express love.

Something else began that same year, though: a sexually abusive relationship with a neighbor. I was an eleven-year-old with a childhood crush that he manipulated to abuse. I felt special that I had this secret as we snuck around his family and mine. My parents were so busy managing the family business that it was easy for me to make excuses to be at his house. I certainly wasn't mature enough to understand the situation as being abusive nor the myriads of feelings as a result of the secret I carried around for the many years it continued. I was confused: Did I feel special or horrible? What I knew for sure was that it was something I needed to keep hidden.

Many years later I shared my story as if it wasn't a big deal with my husband. He recognized it as abuse, even though I had never seen it that way.

My denial was buried deeply until it all boiled up when I was in massage therapy school and also pregnant with my first child. I was in a practice session with fellow classmates, learning to work on the chest and around the pubic bone. Suddenly, I felt something welling up in me and literally ran out of the room. Once in an empty classroom, I began wailing. It came from deep inside me. I opened my mouth and out it poured.

This was the beginning of my realization that I had repressed old feelings in my body, waiting for an outlet to emerge. These feelings felt foreign and painful. Until that moment, I had no idea they even existed.

Later, seeking therapy, breathwork, and emotional release work, I began to recognize the magnitude of this abusive experience. I was fortunate to work with several skilled therapists to support my healing process.

This was undoubtedly the most traumatic experience from my past, one that profoundly influenced my identity. During that period, I developed coping mechanisms I'm still working through more than fifty years later. One of these is turning to food as the best refuge for feeling safe and loved. The extra weight has served as a protective shield to hide behind.

I know, unfortunately, that I am not alone; many others share a similar story. It was the secrecy and the narratives I constructed around it that had stifled me until I was willing to face them head-on. Only when I acknowledged the abuse with complete honesty and sought support was I able to begin healing.

During a period of self-reflection, I admitted that my previous methods of releasing the excessive weight had the strength of a sticky note in a hurricane and realized how ineffective and short-lived they were. Each attempt felt promising initially but quickly unraveled, leaving me back at square one, frustrated and disheartened.

In my vulnerable state, I had an aha moment about an old story I'd told myself for years: Disciplined people are boring. I've always valued spontaneity, believing that variety is the spice of life. This rationale justified my lack of accountability for the food I consumed daily.

Complicating matters, I'd long abandoned dieting, viewing restrictions as punishment that only worked short-term. This fed my resistance to tracking food and being accountable. I wondered how I could maintain my free-spirited zest for life while pursuing my optimal weight.

I also admitted a bad habit of sneaking food. I'd hide that I was eating sweets, perpetuating my long habit of keeping body-related secrets. At the root of all this was an old belief that I deserved to carry extra weight and that it was the only way to feel truly safe.

My willingness to confront these stories has allowed me to make peace with my past, let go of the secrets, and create a loving plan for myself. My success is coming steadily. I've pulled out all the stops as if my life depends on it—because it does. Journaling, affirmations, visualization, and mirror work are now staples of my daily self-care routine.

I know my path will have bumps and setbacks. Sometimes, it's hard to be patient. If I'm being honest, I still fantasize about a magic wand to give me the results I want right now.

Ultimately, I've embraced the health consequences I might face if I don't release this weight. My father passed away too young, just two years older than I am now, due to obesity. I have so much to live for and imagine myself reaching one hundred. The reality is this would be unlikely without making the necessary changes.

My desire to overcome decades of weight issues extends beyond physical health. It's intertwined with the essence of my brand: Choosing Vibrancy. I want to represent myself as someone who defies her age—a role model for aging well, taking on athletic adventures well into old age.

I have a calling to inspire every woman who has faced a roadblock and perhaps almost given up hope. If there's even a glimmer of hope for realizing an audacious goal, I want to be the beacon that says, "You can do it too."

In the end, it's all about rewriting a new story.

Meet **Sherri Danzig**, who boldly pivoted more than three decades ago from a successful career in the food industry to follow her true calling as a wellness professional, neuromuscular therapist, and global wellness entrepreneur. Sherri is the visionary CEO behind Choosing Vibrancy. Her mission is to inspire and educate the world on the power of natural and simple self-care solutions. Through her work, Sherri has touched the lives of thousands, boosting their health and vitality to new heights. She is a lifelong student of both the science and art of personal empowerment. With Sherri's guidance, prepare to embark on your own journey of empowerment and discover the vibrant life that awaits you!

choosingvibrancy.com

THE MESSY MIDDLE

Betty Emrey

I wish I could tell you how this story ends. But I don't know. I'm still in the middle of living it. The messy middle—you know, that place where you've left one phase of your life and are heading into the next. There's hope but not a lot of evidence. It's still too early to know exactly how it's going to turn out, how long it's going to take, or if it's even going to work. I'm not tempted to go backward, but frankly, going forward looks like a big hot mess of unknowns. Some days I feel energized and motivated. I can see my progress. Other days the mix of fear, uncertainty, and fatigue make me wonder if I shouldn't just give in to the fantasy of "early retirement." I've been in similar spaces before. All of us have, right? You can't get from one goal to the next without going through the middle. Some middles are just messier than others.

Part of what makes the middle so messy is that it's kind of boring and lonely. In the very beginning, there is the excitement of starting a new thing—there may be people cheering your decision or maybe even helping you take a few of the first steps. You're buoyed by community—fueled by possibility and butterflies. Then the newness wears off, community recedes back to normal levels, and it's up to you to keep this new thing upright. Which is sometimes just hard work you have to figure out how to sustain. I don't like to talk about how hard life sometimes occurs to me. Maybe you feel the same way. For me, part of it is ego and part is woo-woo and part is Imposter Syndrome. I don't want to be seen as inept. I don't want to be a complainer always bringing the energy down. And I'm certain that other people don't struggle the way I do to get things done.

The more I think about the messy middle, though, the more I think that the majority of our time is actually spent there. Sure, we all hit goals, but those peaks are celebratory blips in the overarching timeline of our lives. Most of the time, we're working toward something. We make plans. We work the plan. And then we deal with the reality of what happens.

When I first became a copywriter, my plan was to work in an agency in Atlanta for a couple of years and then go freelance. Here's what happened, though. Right out of school, instead of getting a job offer in Atlanta, I got one in New York City. New York wasn't on my list, but if you're in advertising, how do you say no to New York? So I shifted my plan to include working in New York for a couple of years, after which I would come back to an agency in Atlanta and *then* go for the freelance career. But New York is a hard place to leave. Every time my apartment lease came due, something interesting was happening. So, I'd stay for "one more year." And before I knew it, I'd been there for seven years.

One of the things that happened while I was living in New York is that I started walking shelter dogs at the ASPCA. It was a way to get my dog fix without the responsibility of actually owning a dog. Before long, I was training new volunteers, and I eventually landed an apprenticeship with one of the trainers there who taught me how to teach dog training classes to the public. In fact, the last time I extended my stay in NYC for "one more year," it was to participate in that apprenticeship.

When I returned to Atlanta, I came back with Madison Avenue copywriting experience and what I thought would be my "retirement career." I got another agency job. I did a little volunteering at the Atlanta Humane Society, and I took my own dog—a chihuahua I had adopted from the ASPCA right before I moved back to Atlanta—to agility classes. That's when I discovered that the training center was looking for a new teacher for puppy kindergarten and basic manners classes. So, I started teaching on the weekends. By this point, my original plan of starting my own freelance career was all but forgotten.

And then I got laid off.

The job, in a small marketing agency, was one I both loved and hated. I loved the people and the work we did. But I didn't fit there creatively. By the time I was laid off, my self-confidence was at an all-time low. In retrospect, I should have left earlier, but I no longer believed I had what it took to be successful anywhere else. Instead, I sucked it up and clung to the routine and the paycheck and the unrealistic hope that it might somehow get better. While no one wants to get laid off, I was profoundly stuck. Losing that job was the best thing that could have ever happened to me. It was finally time for me to resurrect my old dream of freelancing.

Launching my freelance copywriting business was both exciting and terrifying. It was definitely a messy place of fear, doubt, and uncertainty. What if I couldn't find work? What if my clients didn't like the copy I wrote? What if I failed? What then? I forced myself to start reaching out to people to reconnect and let them know what I was up to. Here's what I discovered. A lot of the people I'd worked with over my career were still there, ready and willing to help me make connections, find projects, and get back on my feet. I will always be grateful to them for their support and encouragement. Beyond that, the clients I worked with were actually delighted with the copy I wrote for them. And I had some income from dog training to help tide me over as I transitioned from a staff position to running my own business.

For the next seven years, my copywriting business hummed along. Some years were leaner than others. But at the end of the day, I was able to support myself and write copy for many wonderful clients.

Until this year.

There's something about a period of seven years. Some studies say your cells regenerate every seven years. Human developmental theories claim that people go through major life changes roughly every seven years. Astrologers talk about Saturn's return in seven-year increments which mark various life stages. There's the seven-year itch in relationships. And economists talk about business cycles as lasting approximately seven years.

I suspect I'm on the cusp of one of my seven-year cycles.

At the end of year seven, my business shifted. Clients who had been great for repeat business suddenly dried up. Projects started taking way longer than normal to complete, so paychecks were fewer and farther in between. I started mining my contacts for potential new business and did some cold-pitching. But by the second quarter of the year, I had to take a hard look at what was happening in my business. The reality was I simply wasn't making enough to support myself, and the efforts I'd put in weren't paying off fast enough. It was time for a plan shift.

I took a fresh look at my plans for dog training. I'd been teaching less as my writing business grew. But as my writing work slowed, I started to rethink that ratio. After some serious soul-searching, I decided to scale back on my writing business and focus more on dog training. I've recently taken a staff job at Canine PhD in Decatur, Georgia, where I'd been a contract trainer for fifteen years. This iteration of my plan is basically an accelerated version of my previous "retirement career," only without the retirement. I'm excited about doing more training. But it's been seven years since I've worked in an office. There are a lot of adjustments to make. I'm still early in this transition, so I don't know how this plan is going to work or how this phase of my life and business will ultimately shake out.

I'm in the messy middle.

Being in the middle is uncomfortable. Right now, I'm struggling to figure out who I am in my business. Am I a writer or a dog trainer? Can I choose one? Do I have the focus and energy to be both? I don't know yet. But one thing I do know is that there's no way to get to those answers except through this messy middle. So, one of the things I'm working on is learning how to embrace the discomfort and trust the process.

This is the journey that leads to celebrating those goals. This is where we learn what we're made of and what matters most to us. Ultimately, I know I'm going to be OK, because I've done this before. Even so, I wish I could wrap this story up in a neat, inspiring package where things turn out better than I'd ever imagined. That may actually be the case. Because for all of my plans that went in different directions—almost always the difference was better than what I'd envisioned . . . even if I didn't know it at the time.

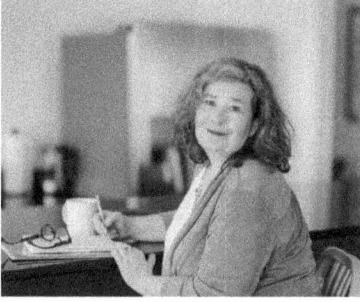

Betty Emrey is an award-winning copywriter and certified dog trainer. She is the owner of Use Your Words Marketing and a certified dog trainer at Canine PhD in Decatur, Georgia. She lives in Atlanta, Georgia, with a Border Collie who graciously forgives her for not having sheep.

useyourwordsmarketing.com

WHAT IF I FLY?

Biviana Franco

"*What if I fall?*" These words have whispered to me countless times when facing the unknown. But the second part of the question has always lifted me: "*Oh but my darling, what if you fly?*"

The first time I read this quote, it felt as though the universe was speaking directly to my heart. Fear, the root of every hesitation and "what if," struck me deeply. But what resonated even more was the power of trying—stepping into the unknown and following your heart, even when it feels impossible. Over the past fifteen years as CEO and founder of Feel Beautiful Today, I've learned that not every leap leads to success. Yet the act of trying, of pushing beyond fear, has enriched me in ways I never imagined. Beyond fear lies a world of possibility, growth, and the most rewarding journey.

Just a few weeks ago, as my husband and I celebrated thirty-one years of marriage, he asked me a question that stopped me in my tracks: "What would you do differently?" I've never been one to dwell on regrets, so instead of looking back critically, I found myself reflecting on the pivotal moments of my life—those when I chose to follow my heart. Each of those decisions, big and small, was guided by a deep passion or a dream that I couldn't ignore. And looking back now, I realize I wouldn't change a thing. The common thread in all those choices was simple: I listened to my heart, even when the path ahead was unclear.

It reminds me of two quotes that perfectly capture my approach to life: "Luck is what happens when preparation meets opportunity," and "Be ready to jump when the train comes by." These statements resonate deeply with me because they underscore the importance of being prepared and seizing the moment when it arrives. Throughout my life, I was unknowingly preparing, building skills, and getting ready for something I couldn't yet see. There was always a sense that something greater was waiting just beyond the horizon. And when the moment came, I was ready to leap, trusting that my heart would lead the way.

This is not by coincidence. I believe there is a Creator, and each of us carries His imprint deep within our souls. The real challenge is being aware enough to recognize the moment when that incredible feeling washes over you—the feeling that you've found your true purpose, the task you were born to fulfill. That realization isn't just a moment of clarity; it's a profound awakening, confirming that everything you've experienced has led you to this point.

Now that you know the quotes and beliefs that have shaped my journey, let me share the story life has written for me. It's a story that began when I was confronted with something that broke my heart. In 2009, my aunt was diagnosed with cancer, and just a few months later, we lost her. My mother, who was by her side throughout the ordeal, shared with me the challenges and pain she witnessed. Each day, during our phone calls between Colombia and the United States, where I now was living, I learned about the emotional and physical toll cancer takes on both patients and their caregivers.

Until then, cancer was something distant for me. As a child, I didn't know anyone with cancer. It wasn't until I was an adult that I started hearing more frequently about people being diagnosed or passing away. But even then, I was unaware of the deep, complex needs of those facing this battle. Then, after my aunt passed, two friends around my age were diagnosed with cancer, and that's when I began to truly see and understand the life-altering impact of it. What struck me most was the emotional toll—the profound changes and challenges my friends faced as they fought this relentless disease.

A question took root in my heart: *What can I do?* I wasn't a doctor or a cook—my culinary skills were limited to boiling eggs. But I could paint; I could create. With a degree in design and five years of experience in drawing and painting, art had always been my passion, a way to make sense of the world. I was captivated by art's symbolism and its window into cultures, history, and the human soul.

As I searched for ways to help cancer patients, a new question arose: *Could art be my way to pour love and hope into their lives?* My previous work with nonprofits supporting health challenges revealed that art could be more than just creativity—it could be a powerful tool for healing. I had discovered creativity's true power, not merely as self-expression but as a means of transformation and healing. Art could uplift, providing refuge from mental battles, and this resonated deeply with me. Seeing art help others navigate their struggles reaffirmed my belief in its ability to drive social change and enhance well-being. Art became more than a passion; it became my way of making a tangible difference in the world.

Reflecting on the quotes that guided me, I knew fear had to be cast aside. I had no business plan, no budget—just a heart full of desire to make a difference. My preparation? Yes, I studied art and design, but what truly prepared me were those Fridays spent serving in marginalized areas of Bogotá during high school. Witnessing social injustices and a struggling community made me realize that every step in my life had led to this moment. Though I lacked all the answers, I had the passion, drive, and belief that this was my path. Fear couldn't stand in the way. I didn't overthink—I just did it.

And so, just as the quote suggests, the train passed by, and I jumped on. I started by creating a service project in the community, which within a few months blossomed into a full-fledged movement. Soon after, some of my closest friends encouraged me to consider formalizing this into a nonprofit organization. It's been fifteen years since that pivotal moment, and with the support of thousands and an incredible team of volunteers working shoulder to shoulder, we have launched ten arts-in-health programs, impacting more than seventeen thousand patients in Georgia. Our programs are delivered to cancer centers at no cost to patients and are all aimed at supporting the well-being of those battling cancer. The journey has been nothing short of transformative, and it's been a blessing to see how the arts can profoundly impact lives.

"Oh but my darling, what if you fly?" This question has become a mantra in my life. And let me tell you, while fear was definitely in the mix, it didn't stand a chance against my passion and determination. Along the way, I've picked up some valuable lessons about life, myself, others, and God. For instance, I discovered I was able to give a public speech, with a Latin accent as unmistakable as a tango step. Now, fifteen years after launching Feel Beautiful Today, even though my accent might still be dancing around, my ability to think and speak clearly is more polished than ever. I've learned several valuable lessons, such as focusing on the positives rather than the rejections. Prayer has proven powerful, providing timely support when I was at my lowest. These experiences have deepened my understanding of resilience and faith. Even though my certifications and training courses seemed endless, I've come to enjoy the continual growth. I love looking back and seeing how I've improved or picked up new skills that make the work easier, or at least more secure. This way, at any point in the process, I can jump in and get the job done.

When Marie Fratoni invited me to be part of this book, I was thrilled at the chance to inspire a new generation of women. My heart is full, knowing that I've had the chance to give life to my ideas. I hope this chapter prompts someone to ask, "What if I fly?" Even when my mom was diagnosed with cancer eight years ago, I channeled my sadness into my work with renewed determination, aiming to make a difference for those like her navigating cancer.

Reflecting on this journey fills me with gratitude and purpose. Each challenge, leap of faith, and doubt has been a step toward something greater. My two sons have been my constant motivation. I hope they remember how I poured my heart into following my dreams and always tried to make a positive impact.

The lessons I've learned affirm the power of giving back while pursuing one's passion with dedication. To those reading this, I hope my story inspires you to confront your own "what ifs" with courage. The path may be uncertain, but within each of us lies the potential to create something beautiful. Embrace the fear, trust your heart, and take the leap—because even if the journey begins with a fall, it can lead to extraordinary heights.

Biviana "Bivi" Franco is the visionary behind Feel Beautiful Today, a nonprofit in Atlanta, Georgia. Originally from Colombia, Bivi's love for art led her to earn a degree in fashion design, graduating magna cum laude, and to study classical art, drawing, and photography. In 2010, after losing her aunt to cancer and seeing friends struggle with the disease, she founded Feel Beautiful Today to provide hope and encouragement to cancer patients through art. Her nonprofit has impacted more than seventeen thousand oncology patients in Georgia. Bivi's faith and her mother's cancer diagnosis in 2015 deepened her commitment, making art a powerful tool for connection and inspiration.

feelbeautifultoday.org

THE DIFFERENCE A JOB MAKES

Susan Gall-Quettan

November 4, 1968—the day before my fourth birthday. I was riding in the car with my parents. We were driving down the streets of Trinidad and Tobago, and I was excitedly looking out the window and counting cars as they passed by. I had no idea that we were heading to the airport. I didn't know that my dad had lost his job, or that my mom had found a job in New York as a nanny for a family with kids around my age. When we arrived at the airport, my mom kissed my dad and me goodbye and disappeared. One moment I had a mom, and the next moment she was gone.

Two years later, my dad and I were walking down the street together. He was holding my hand and was carrying a piece of luggage in his other hand. Suddenly, I heard something drop and looked over to find my clothes on the ground. As he quickly threw them back into the suitcase, I wondered, *Why does my dad have my clothes?*

Ten minutes later, we arrived at my mother's parents' home. My dad put down my suitcase, waved goodbye, and walked away. As I looked at my grandparents' house, I saw broken windows, a leaky roof, and splintered floorboards. Inside I discovered there was no electricity and no running water. *Why did he leave me here?* I start counting the people who were living in the house, and when I realized that I would be the ninth person, I got sad and quiet.

Daily life was challenging, to say the least. Breakfast sometimes consisted of one egg and one slice of bread to share among the nine of us. No one in that home had a regular job, so there was never enough money to buy food, pay bills, or make repairs. I quickly realized that a job was not something trivial; at times it was a matter of life or death, of starving or thriving.

Today, I believe that creating jobs is the most important thing I can do to create a fulfilled life for others. Let me tell you why having a job has such a major impact on our day-to-day lives.

A Job Leads to a Fulfilled Life

People who are unemployed experience about 30 percent more negative emotional experiences in their day-to-day lives. Always worrying about where the next dollar will come from to buy food, pay rent, and educate their children creates stress and anxiety. Unemployment also has a significant impact on a person's physical health. Being unemployed is a highly stressful situation, so it may cause stress-related health issues such as headaches, high blood pressure, diabetes, heart disease, and back pain. And in most cases, no job means no health insurance to get medical care. It sucks when you cannot even provide the basic needs for yourself and family—but it's life-transforming when you can!

Life with my grandparents was hard since no one had a regular job. Two years after my mom left, she came back to Trinidad to visit, bringing a suitcase filled with clothes for me. She purchased all the food I wanted for the three weeks she was in Trinidad. For those three weeks, I lacked nothing, and life was great. During those three weeks, I was able to experience the difference her job made in my life. I lived a fulfilled life while she was there, but then she left, and it was back to normal for me, and I hated it.

These visits continued for several years. Finally, when I was sixteen, I asked myself, "How can I continue to live a life of lack?" That led to an aha moment: **Be willing to take actions toward having a fulfilled life**. I could find a way to move to America with my mom, or I could stay in Trinidad and exist like my other family members, sitting around idle and jobless and complaining all the time.

Guess what I chose? I found a way to join her in Miami so I could begin to pursue my dreams. Life wasn't great in Miami. My mom had a job, but she was married to an alcoholic who often made our life miserable, but he had a job as an air conditioner mechanic with the University of Miami, and as an employee, his children could attend the University of Miami for free.

My mom told me that my "job" was to go to the University of Miami and graduate. "With an education," she said, "you will always be able to take care of yourself." My mom stayed with my alcoholic stepfather and put up with all it takes to live with an alcoholic just so I could get that free education.

I was determined to graduate even though I found myself in a world very different than what I was used to. In this world of rich White and Hispanic students, I felt less than, but I knew this was my access to become self-sufficient. Therefore, I played full out in the midst of all the challenges I faced. And I did it! I graduated, and now I could buy and eat a whole egg!

So now what? What would do I do with this experience?

Pursuing Dreams and Creating Jobs

Eighteen years later, my dream is fulfilled. I became an entrepreneur and now I create jobs for others. In my company, I've created jobs for fifty-eight people and counting—jobs that allow my employees to pay their bills, feed and educate their children, and pursue their own dreams.

Being an entrepreneur is not easy. It takes courage and adaptability. The world of work is set to go through major changes in the coming years. Even today 90 percent of jobs in the United States are created by small businesses like yours and mine. How are we going to keep creating jobs?

I believe it's by being committed to job creation. This commitment takes courage. You must move past your fear of failure, be resilient, unstoppable, and be willing to overcome any challenges that come your way. When you experience the value and the difference a job makes, you just want to help create more jobs. I was able to experience an abundance of food and clothes because of my mother's job, and I was able to get an education that led to being an employer because of my stepfather's job. Now, as a business owner, I've seen and experienced the difference a job makes in the lives of others. I have helped employees move from living in their cars to living in four-bedroom homes with garages. I've seen how having a job allows them to pay to educate themselves and move on to better jobs, purchase homes and new cars, and I've witnessed the pride and joy they experience from these accomplishments. The difference creating jobs makes brings me such joy.

My grandparents' house that I referred to at the beginning of this chapter has been remodeled too. It now has running water, electricity, internet, a modern, state-of-the-art kitchen, five bathrooms, and seven bedrooms. And all this was accomplished by hiring people in the local community. That's the difference my job has made! My dream being fulfilled creates others' dreams being fulfilled! What a way to live a fulfilled life!

Will you join me in creating one new job this year for someone else?

Susan Gall-Quettan is the co-founder and chief executive officer of QM3 Utility Services. She has led a concerted effort across all levels of the organization to optimize the business for the current natural gas integrity management environment while staying true to the fundamentals that have been foundational to the company's accelerated growth and innovation over the past nineteen years. At QM3, we practice doing 1 percent better in everything we do, and we always keep our vision in mind: "Protect, Contribute, and Grow . . . Continuously." Our employees are our most valuable assets, and this produces a high level of employee satisfaction.

qm3us.com

NAVIGATING THE CHASM OF CLINICAL DEPRESSION

Donna D. Hill, FLMI

It was rare in my childhood to see my daddy angry, but one day, when I was thirteen years old, he was furious. He had just learned that I was scheduled to go on a church outing to the local water park the next day, but I was refusing to go because I was sure no one liked me, and I knew I would be miserable. He sat me down and very gently informed me that I was just as good as anyone else. He pointed out that I had straight As in school, got glowing remarks from teachers, and had several close friends. There was no reason for me to feel inferior or unpopular.

To make my daddy proud, I bucked up my pride and went on the outing. The result of Daddy's pep talk that day had much further-reaching consequences than getting me to go on that outing (where, of course, I had a great time). His words of encouragement bolstered me throughout my life when I was feeling unworthy and unloved. It was an underpinning I credit with my survival.

For the first fifty years of my life, I drifted, unmoored and often unfocused. I married my high school sweetheart, but after four-and-a-half months of marriage, he came home one day and said he didn't like being married and was moving back in with his mother. I was devastated and briefly contemplated suicide. When one of my sister's in-laws, who lived in Atlanta, heard of my situation, they called me and invited me to leave my home state of Alabama and live with them while I found my footing. To this day, I don't know where I got the courage to go, but I did.

During my first few months in Atlanta, I drifted from job to job, never staying anywhere long. I quit a few of them but was usually dismissed for not being engaged with the job enough to do it well. I still had very little belief in my value. After almost a year living alone, I was introduced to Steve, and we eventually married. Having someone in my life gave me some purpose and direction.

I now had a more stable personal life, but I still struggled with my career. You can go into any fifth grade classroom and ask the students what they want to do when they grow up, and not one of them will say, "I want to be an insurance agent," and I was no exception. I just happened to land a job as office manager in a regional insurance office for a large health insurance carrier. It was something I was good at and enjoyed doing. I took on many of the manager's responsibilities and made myself invaluable. During this time, I obtained my Fellow of the Life Management Institute (FLMI) designation, and I eventually became the first female—and the first non-degreed—regional sales executive in that company.

I was suffering from clinical depression, although I didn't know it at the time, but I tempered it with positive motivation and affirmations. I discovered the philosophies of great motivators like Jack Canfield, Zig Ziglar, Les Brown, and Tony Robbins. Interestingly, these authors and many others I have studied all basically say the same thing. It boils down to an understanding that our brains believe and act on the information we feed them. If that is a positive affirmation, our attitude will reflect that. Of course, the inverse is also true.

In the ensuing years, I joined and volunteered for the National Association of Health Underwriters (now the National Association of Benefits and Insurance Professionals), and in 2000-2001, I served as the president of the state chapter. I was invited to chair several committees on the national level. By anyone's estimation, my career was a success, yet I still felt like an imposter. Deep down, I still felt I was unworthy and unloved despite all the evidence to the contrary. Continual feeding on positive affirmation was all that kept my head above water.

In 2009, my carefully built underpinnings started to unravel. By then I owned a successful insurance agency specializing in health insurance plans for trucking companies. The economic downturn that began in 2008 wiped out my three largest clients. My business partner of eight years decided to retire. I was diagnosed with renal cell carcinoma. It was too much. I closed my agency and was once again adrift.

I increasingly spent time in bed, grew more and more irritable with my husband and son, and had little belief in my ability to improve my situation. And then God placed an amazing woman in my path, and this literally saved me. An educator at the highest levels, she continues to inspire me, and she is a true friend. She was not afraid to step in where she saw a need. She had watched me suffer enough and told me in no uncertain terms that I clearly suffered from clinical depression, probably ADD, and possibly a mood disorder. She ordered me to come to my senses and seek professional help.

I was having frequent crying jags and barely functioning at this point, so I decided I had nothing to lose and consulted a doctor. We worked through my symptoms and settled on a combination of drugs that worked an overnight miracle. These drugs are not supposed to work overnight, but I was the exception. Within forty-eight hours, I had a nearly complete turnaround in my outlook and attitude. I started looking for a new direction for my career and began to mend the relationships I had damaged with my unhappiness and irritability.

My son, who had a psychology degree, understood my turnaround and supported it wholeheartedly. My husband was slower to get there. The depths of my depression had deteriorated our marriage to the point he had turned away from the relationship. He was not willing to risk believing that things were fundamentally different now or that these changes would last. Thankfully, as time passed and I remained upbeat and focused, the closeness and affection we had once experienced returned.

I found purpose and direction in ways I had never experienced, and he came to believe in me again.

That was in 2012. It is now 2024. In the intervening years I have:

- Joined an insurance agency that shares my values and goals and became a director.
- Discovered that helping seniors navigate the complex world of Medicare is what I am meant to be doing, and I love doing it.
- Joined a Rotary Club and found that "Service Above Self" is a way of life that fulfills me in ways I never knew I needed.
- Realized that not only am I not unloved, but I have an army of friends who would come if I called, and even a few who would take a bullet for me.
- Rebuilt my marriage so it is stronger than ever. We will soon celebrate our fiftieth wedding anniversary.
- Survived, side by side with my husband, the illness and death of our only child from a pernicious infection without falling back into the chasm. This was the biggest challenge I faced, and I was on guard for any signs of the return of debilitating depression. A lifetime of teaching myself that my life is governed not by what happens to me, but how I react to what happens to me, pulled me through the grieving process.
- Grown stronger than ever in my faith and my belief that I am made in God's image, and He has my back.

If you have doubts about whether you are good enough, struggle to get out of bed in the morning, or find yourself drifting without purpose, I encourage you to consult a physician about the possibility you are experiencing clinical depression. This is a disease, not a failure. There is no shame, and there should be no hesitation in seeking treatment. Clinical depression is a chemical imbalance that is fully treatable. You can overcome it and soar to astounding heights, so please seek help and support!

Donna D. Hill, FLMI, is the director of Individual and Senior Markets and the compliance director for E2E Benefits Services in Duluth, Georgia. Her passion is guiding seniors through the complex world of Medicare. She is an active member of the National Association of Benefits and Insurance Professionals and frequently speaks to civic and business groups on Medicare issues. She lives in Lilburn, Georgia, with her husband, Steve, and five rescue dogs.

DON'T LET WHAT YOU CAN'T DO KEEP YOU FROM WHAT YOU CAN!

Felicia Morris

Imagine waking up in a hospital bed with a multitude of tubes and wires from head to toe. Machines are beeping and a distinguished-looking doctor is standing at the foot of the bed, reading a chart. He says, "Well, we have some good news! You don't have gonorrhea, syphilis, or AIDS."

That was my situation. Immediately, I thought, *I don't know where I am. I don't know who you are, but I know one thing—that is GOOD news!*

Over the next several days, I would learn that I had suffered a debilitating grand mal seizure brought on by the swelling of ten lesions in my brain. The seizure left me partially paralyzed on my right side and laid to waste my short-term memory and cognitive abilities.

The doctors poked, prodded, and drilled to find the source of the lesions, but they found none. Ultimately, they diagnosed me with multiple sclerosis, settled on a treatment of heavy IV steroids and weekly interferon injections to shrink the lesions, and released me after three weeks in ICU to start my lifelong journey in a new reality.

Personally, I wasn't concerned about the source of the lesions. I simply wanted to know how to put all of this in reverse, so I could get back to being "successful."

Before I woke up that day, I was a thirty-seven-year-old former Miss Georgia's Miss Congeniality, a big-seven stockbroker, and a national award-winning membership director for large trade organizations. I sat on the board of my profession's association, regularly spoke to large audiences, worked with and played golf with movers and shakers, AND took "good care" of my mother.

Now What?

What am I going to do? I'm grateful to be alive, BUT I'm single, can barely walk, speak in complete sentences, write, type, add, or subtract.

First, I was depressed. I realized quickly that only made it all seem worse.

Next, perseverance! I would get back to work!

What are my staff members' names again? What year is it? Walking to my assistant's office to read her name plate on the door, I knew this wasn't workable for anyone!

Finally, acceptance. It was time to use that personal disability policy that I had, by the grace of God, personally funded when I was a stockbroker and focus on healing.

That was 1999.

What I've Learned

The year 2024 marks the twenty-fifth anniversary of that medical event. It has been and continues to be an amazing journey to create a fully self-expressed life while dealing powerfully with the residual mental symptoms of the seizure and keeping the progression of multiple sclerosis (and any other lurking, unwanted condition) at bay.

The first of many, many, many transformations happened within days of coming home from the hospital:

I'm lying in my bed at home, reflecting on my "things"—nice clothes, beautiful big-city apartment, nice car, two legs that slowly shuffle to the bathroom, which seems like a mile away, and memories of numerous failed relationships. Suddenly, all the "stuff" seems so pointless and unnecessary. I think of Mother Teresa. She cared so little about worldly possessions and lived an amazing life of service that made a difference for thousands of poor, blind, disabled, and aged in India. *When I get better, I'm going to be more like her*, I think. *Life is a miraculous gift and I've been wasting it chasing the "stuff."*

The Turning Point

Three years after the seizure, I was back at my neurologist's office, alone in the waiting room. I overhear the MRI rep inviting my doctor's assistant to an event at Landmark's Training and Development Center. I thought, *I've heard of that and maybe this is the time go do their class.* So, I politely asked if I could come along.

The Landmark Forum is an amazing weekend adventure to personal discovery—an opportunity to be an observer of your life. It's a chance to see the decisions you made up about life, the impact those decisions have on you (and everyone around you), and an opportunity to "clear the board" so you can create newly ANYTHING you want.

During the course, there are numerous conversations. One of them focuses on three turning points in every person's life. When I did the exercise, I saw that at six years old, I decided I had to be smart so Dad wouldn't be mad; at thirteen, I had to do what everyone else wants to do so I could fit in; and at twenty-two, I had to be ridiculously successful to financially help my mom. When you put those together, what do you get? An arrogant, people-pleasing control freak. From ages fifteen to thirty-seven, I ran the hamster wheel of life hard—constantly strategizing to prove I was smarter, faster, and better than you! No wonder I wound up in ICU!

With this discovery, I saw that I have a choice, and I chose to recreate myself as an enthusiastic, inspiring, energizing bunny with a long list of apologies to make, starting with Mom.

Mom wasn't so excited about my new discovery. We had become comfortable in our dysfunctional, backward relationship. I said, "Mom, I love you and I apologize that I have been acting like you need me to tell you how to live your life. I'm not going anywhere, but starting now, I give up that I know better than you. If you want my opinion, I'll wait for you to ask!" It took time, but our friendship flourished, and Mom started making new choices for herself. We had eight years as best friends; we traveled and played cards together and took care of each other until she passed.

It Is Possible

The level of peace that has permeated my life since the Landmark Forum is amazing. I continue to participate in numerous courses and develop my leadership skills to share with others that success without peace and community is not success. Sacrificing either of them leads to being poor in your health, happiness, or finances. What is required is a willingness to authentically be of service to others and honor your promises. Simply stopping the people-pleasing created the opportunity for me discover my own creativity, like painting, and to work exercise into my days. Within two years of completing the Forum, I was able to transition to holistic practices to manage the majority of my pain and fatigue issues as I continued my quest to reverse the damage I did in my arrogant, workaholic, hamster-running years.

One other thing about being arrogant. Back in the day, at the height of my career, I was "nice" and "funny" to everyone, but if you weren't interested or aligned with what I was up to, you were mostly invisible to me, and heaven forbid if I decided you weren't "smart."

There's nothing quite like being mentally and physically struck down to give you a new perspective. For many years, I struggled to think of a word, stumbled in my speaking, moved incredibly slowly, and struggled to stay awake. It was frustrating for everyone and dramatically impacted my confidence, but it gave me a new perspective on compassion. You never know what others are dealing with and the difference your being compassionate can make. No one is great at everything, but everyone is great at something! Be kind. Find the gold in everyone.

Wake Up!

Over these last twenty-five years, the biggest challenge has been the fatigue. Even when it looks like I'm alert, I'm thinking about taking a nap. Top it off with a pandemic and being over sixty . . . you get the picture. I gained the "COVID 20" during the shutdown (on top of already being twenty-five pounds overweight), and the pain in my legs returned. Time to recreate the possibility of being an enthusiastic, inspiring, energizing bunny! Standing in that possibility, I joined my family in each of us losing forty pounds, went back to physical therapy, and started considering stem cell injections (estimated cost: $12,000; failure rate: 30 percent). Then I heard about a groundbreaking invention: an affordable one-inch patch that wakes up your own stem cells and causes your body to regenerate from within. *Why not try it?* I thought.

The results have been shocking. The chronic fatigue lifted! I'm AWAKE! I have a sense of well-being I haven't experienced since my early thirties! I'm excited to discover what's next in a world where anything is possible, and I hope you are too! Keep creating, keep learning, and don't let what you can't do keep you from what you can!

© 2024 Claude A. Loma-Solet

An advocate for health, wealth, and transformation, **Felicia Morris** lives in Decatur, Georgia, with her entrepreneurial, television drama writer life partner, Marjorie McRae, and their adorable six-pound Pomeranian, Mia Giada!

Retired from years of membership consulting and people-pleasing, Felicia is a leader in the Landmark Self Expression and Leadership Academy. She is a community builder, dedicating her time to inspiring others to create a life they love by sharing the practices and products that have been invaluable in creating hers!

info@reverse2day.com

A JOURNEY OF
CONNECTIONS

Paige Nathan

Life can only be understood backwards, but it must be lived forwards.
—Soren Kierkegaard

Growing up surrounded by curiosity and exploration, my childhood was a vibrant mix of experiences focused on making connections. Raised as an only child by parents who valued culture and diversity, my early years were filled with art and food festivals, antique shows, and international dinner guests. My dad was a lifelong learner with many interests, and my mom was an accomplished fundraiser and natural networker. This dynamic duo instilled in me a sense of wonder, community, and a love of connecting with others.

In the 1980s, I had an idea to create a service that would connect people and food. Long before the internet, I dreamt of a concierge service offering personalized assistance to food enthusiasts. Years later, this blossomed into a vibrant venture: a food truck booking company. Some may call it luck or kismet, but I know it was the result of connecting the dots of my experiences, strengths, and desires along with meeting the right people at the right time and being open to taking the risk to become an entrepreneur.

Although it took decades for my dream to materialize, the journey taught me the power of patience, perseverance, and following one's passion. Food with Purpose, rebranded in 2020 as Simply Food Trucks, was born from these lifelong lessons, demonstrating that every experience and connection has the potential to spark something extraordinary.

Global Adventures

It all began with a transformative study abroad experience in Spain during college, igniting a lifelong passion for travel. Dining at a Michelin-starred restaurant and savoring a meal at Casa Botin in Madrid, one of the oldest restaurants in the world, were unforgettable culinary highlights.

As college graduation approached, I was captivated by the idea of moving to London for a year. This was before Google, email, and cell phones. Travel magazines were my inspiration, and I found a London-based publishing company on the masthead of *Travel and Leisure* magazine. With the serendipity of timing and the boldness of no risk, no reward, I invited myself to stay with a friend's family during spring break to meet with the company's owner, and I was able to secure a position upon graduation.

I thoroughly enjoyed promoting UK tourism to the US, and I reveled in exploring the country's rich history and culture. High tea at Brown's Hotel, the opulence of Harrod's Food Halls, and working near Covent Garden were among the many highlights of my London adventure.

My curiosity then led me to Southeast Asia, where I immersed myself in Buddhism and the rich cultures of India, Nepal, Thailand, Myanmar, and Indonesia. I trekked the Himalayas, dipped my toes in the Ganges River, and met a Balinese princess. What I initially planned to be a six-week trip turned into an eight-month odyssey, thanks to a network of travelers and my mom's devoted connections. Of course, street food and exotic treats were a big part of these rich experiences along with finding fancy hotels for a swim or a cocktail.

Returning stateside, I settled in Washington, D.C., a hub of international opportunities. There, I found my calling with Youth For

Understanding International Exchange, matching students from the former Soviet Union with American host families. This culminated in a memorable visit to Moscow, where I saw the city through the eyes of a local family.

Through these global adventures, I learned invaluable lessons about adaptability, cultural appreciation, and the importance of forging meaningful connections. Experiencing firsthand diverse cuisines and cultures deepened my understanding of the world and sharpened my ability to connect with people from all walks of life. These experiences taught me that every journey, whether across continents or within our communities, holds lessons that can apply to one's business. By embracing diversity, nurturing relationships, and maintaining an open mind, I found that the essence of successful entrepreneurship lies in these values.

Pathways of Purpose

By 1999, I had married, become a mother, and was living in New Orleans. After a stint as a stay-at-home mom, I craved deeper community connections and longed to immerse myself in the vibrant local culture. Volunteering proved to be a gateway to new opportunities, which led me to become the executive director of Hillel: the Foundation for Jewish Campus Life at Tulane University.

Fundraising—or as I have termed it, friend-raising—has allowed me to network with alumni, parents, and donors nationwide, aligning our passion for Jewish student identity and leadership. My children, Matthew and Daniel, spent their early years immersed in this vibrant community, blending my personal and professional lives seamlessly.

In New Orleans, I discovered the profound impact of community and collaboration. Volunteering opened doors to meaningful roles that allowed me to serve others while honing my leadership skills. My time at Hillel taught me the power of networking and the importance of aligning people's passions with shared goals. Embracing collaboration and recognizing the strengths of others were pivotal lessons.

Transforming Taste

After Hurricane Katrina in 2005, my family relocated to Atlanta, where a serendipitous encounter at The Cook's Warehouse reignited my passion for culinary exploration. I had done a fair bit of volunteering and gig work with several food festivals and chef-driven dinner fundraisers. In fact, one my mentors told me I should call my company Connecting the Dots. One evening, my family and I came upon a new food truck park, and an epiphany struck! This was an amazing and vibrant nexus of food, community, and culture—Indian, Argentinian, Asian, and New Orleans cuisines intermingled, each truck with its own story. And I wanted to be a part of it!

Fortuitously, I connected with three entrepreneurs who had started the first food truck commissary in Atlanta, specializing in food truck management and bookings. With my networking and event management skills, I became their bridge to the corporate world. The fresh concept of food trucks took off with event planners, and I began to amass a following. The owners moved on to other pursuits, and soon after, my food truck business was born.

While my company was successfully rolling along (pun intended), March 2020 brought everything, including my business, to a sudden halt. My dad became very ill, so I spent several months in Baltimore with him and my mom. He was as worried about the future as I was; the unknown was very unsettling and scary for both my livelihood and my passion.

During the pandemic, while many were working from home, food trucks remained a beloved staple. Without corporate business, we pivoted to support first responders and local neighborhoods, although this was not sustainable as a business model. Then, in the spring of 2021, a game-changing email arrived: a health and wellness company was planning an event for ten thousand guests in July. To say this reignited my company is an understatement. We mobilized more than forty food trucks and caterers to serve healthy, international cuisine to the enthusiastic attendees. My dad, who had passed away the previous October, was undoubtedly smiling down on me, proud of the resilience and revival of the business we both cared so deeply about.

Life Lessons Along the Way

The Power of Connections—True happiness lies in the connections we forge and the lives we touch. In a fragmented world, these connections weave us together, fostering a sense of belonging and joy.

Nurturing Relationships—Nurturing meaningful relationships goes beyond transactional interactions. It involves building trust, empathy, and mutual respect with customers, partners, and vendors. Investing in these relationships leads to long-term loyalty, repeat business, and valuable referrals.

Making a Difference—Always going back to my core of connection, volunteerism, and community, these values remain vibrant and alive today through our work with Simply Food Trucks and our philanthropic arm, Simply Giving. We actively partner with food-related organizations, embodying our mission of "food with purpose" by giving back and making a positive impact on our community.

The Art of Open-Mindedness—Staying open to new possibilities requires a mindset of curiosity and adaptability. Continuously seeking opportunities for growth, whether through exploring new markets, adopting emerging technologies, or adapting to a new business model, is essential.

Right People, Right Roles—Getting the right people on board and placing them in the right roles is more art than science. I am incredibly fortunate to have a diverse and collaborative team that brings unique strengths and perspectives to the table. This diversity not only enriches our company culture but also drives innovation and creativity in our operations.

The Reward of Perseverance—Maintaining perseverance and determination is invaluable. Each challenge has been an opportunity for growth, teaching me to find new ways to approach situations, pause and reflect, and seek input from others.

Simply Food Trucks thrives because I continue to embody these principles while creating meaningful culinary experiences that unite communities and drive positive impact. As I continue on this journey, I remain committed to these core values, knowing they can inspire and guide others in their entrepreneurial endeavors.

A special thank you to my husband, Rob, who continues to support and inspire me.

Paige Nathan is the founder of Simply Food Trucks, which specializes in organizing seamless and delicious events for corporate meeting planners, businesses, film production companies, professional sports teams, and nonprofit organizations around the country. Paige is a board member of Les Dames d'Escoffier International, Meeting Planners International, and Society of Incentive Travel Executives.

simplyfoodtrucks.com

DON'T UNDERESTIMATE YOURSELF

Karen Osborne

At twenty-six, I found myself unable to find employment in the interior design industry as the country was in a recession. Rather than wallow, I decided to take a bold leap and start my own business. I was somewhat excited but mostly scared at the thought of this new venture—I knew I was facing formidable odds. According to the U.S. Bureau of Labor Statistics, approximately 20 percent of new businesses fail during the first two years, 45 percent during the first five years, and 65 percent during the first ten years. I couldn't help but feel like I was diving headfirst into the deep end.

A few months in, I made a gutsy move from my home office to a commercial space. Now, I needed help to manage walk-ins and deliveries. Soon, my first assistant came on board, adding to my growing overhead and responsibilities.

When I was first deciding whether I wanted to become an interior designer, I interviewed a local designer about her experience. She told me something I've never forgotten: "To be successful in this business, you have to be really good."

How did I know if I would be really good? For many years, I was in pursuit of that answer.

I didn't get the answer to that question until years later. Why? Despite having numerous satisfied clients, winning multiple project bids, and earning several awards, that burning question persisted. It took many years to understand that the answer wasn't found where I had been looking.

I learned that there was much more to my endeavor. Early in my career, when I went to someone's home for interior design work, I found that a lot of clients wanted to talk and get to know me first. Some wanted to share details of their life as if I were their best friend. I would feel impatient and annoyed because I wanted to get right to work, and they wanted to talk!

It finally hit me! There was a human component, a need for connection and relatedness that I was oblivious to as a twenty-six-year-old. Little did I know that this realization would become the foundation of my success and my fulfillment. It guided me in interacting with clients, colleagues, and employees. I saw that being a "good" interior designer was only part of the whole picture.

Throughout my journey, I've learned that relationships are at the heart of a successful business. By focusing on creating a work environment that is adaptable to working moms and listening to those around me for what matters to them, I've established a great place to work and a foundation to foster strong client relationships. I am confident in my skills as a designer, but the relationships formed through my work have truly enriched my life. Embracing this journey has allowed me to live out my passion for model home merchandising.

I dedicated myself to further growth through participation in personal training and development programs and made it my mission to give back to others and transform communities.

Through this work, I created a deeply personal nonprofit project: "Cailyn's Promise" in memory of a friend's three-year-old daughter who bravely fought and succumbed to brain cancer. Two close friends became my co-chairs, and off we went, utilizing each of our very unique talents. We began with a bold idea: a fashion show fundraiser to provide resources for vulnerable infants at Okoa Refuge, an orphanage in Uganda that Cailyn's family supported. While setting out to raise five thousand dollars was both a challenge and a heartfelt mission, Cailyn's spirit and resilience continued to guide us. We moved mountains and put together a fashion show for two hundred guests in just three-and-a-half months.

I invited Cailyn's parents to join us at the fashion show, and they accepted! The night before the fundraiser, Cailyn's mom called me. She said that knowing I was honoring her daughter's life was the light in her darkness every day. I was deeply moved by her words and blown away that I got to help a young mother navigate her grief. In that moment, I felt a profound connection to my purpose.

Over two years and through the dedication of volunteers, sponsors, and attendees, we raised more than $57,000, including a generous matching contribution from a church in Jacksonville, Florida, that supports the Okoa mission. With these funds, the vision of establishing a medical clinic in Uganda became a reality.

Witnessing this transformation unfold was profoundly gratifying; however, nothing compared to the moment when I saw the medical clinic in person. The words "In Memory of Cailyn Nelson —Okoa Medical Clinic" adorned the building, which was painted in Cailyn's favorite colors. It is a memory that will forever resonate with me, serving as a testament to love, dedication, and a poignant reminder of Cailyn's legacy.

The clinic, initially starting out as a modest facility, has since evolved beyond expectations. In 2023, after additional generous donations from the Okoa team supporters, the Okoa House of Joy Medical Clinic was upgraded to hospital status. It now proudly stands as a hospital comprising two buildings, with crucial services such as labor and delivery care and a full malnutrition ward now available.

Reflecting on this journey, I realize how I had underestimated myself at the onset. Initially believing that raising five thousand dollars was the extent of what I could achieve, I now see the immense power of determination and collective effort. It's a testament to the potential within each of us to effect meaningful change and create lasting impact in the world, one step at a time.

A few short years later, I never imagined that my own life would take a tragic turn. My husband and I had always tried to create a loving and supportive environment for our three children. Our eldest child, Justin, had always been extremely generous, found laughter in many things, and loved fiercely. Unfortunately, he also often struggled with his emotions, which were deeply tied to his own self-condemnation. As he got older, Justin began to battle depression and anxiety.

He found solace in drugs as a way to numb his pain. His experimentation quickly spiraled into addiction. Once a sweet, giving, and loving young boy, he became consumed by his dependency. We did everything we knew to do, seeking therapy, medication, rehabs, tough love at times, and help in crisis situations, but nothing seemed to bring him peace.

The impact on the family was profound. Our marriage became strained under the weight of our son's addiction. Our conversations became dominated by worry, each of us grappling with feelings of guilt and helplessness.

Despite our efforts, Justin's battle with addiction ended tragically when he overdosed in 2019 at the age of twenty-three. Our entire family plunged into a deep well of grief, all in our own ways, struggling to comprehend a world without him. The weeks and months following Justin's death were the darkest. The house felt emptier—Justin's absence a constant, painful reminder of our loss. Holidays and family gatherings, once joyful, became occasions marked by an empty chair and an ever-looming sadness.

Persevering after the loss of a child is a profound challenge. How could we ever be whole again? The transition from a family of five to four was stark and painful. This heart-wrenching experience impacted every member of the family uniquely, reshaping our lives and relationships. We each had to navigate our own sorrow and trauma while trying to support one another.

As time went by, we learned that moving forward didn't mean leaving Justin behind. We speak about him often, sharing memories and celebrating his life rather than focusing on losing him. We still allow ourselves to feel the waves of sadness, knowing that healing is not linear and that some days are still harder than others. By continuing with our own work, pursuing personal passions, and nurturing one another, our family has integrated our loss into our lives, creating a new narrative that includes the memory of a beloved son, brother, and grandson.

Gradually, we have found ways to honor Justin's memory, such as developing a phone application with the help of a magnificent team and many donors. This app, designed to keep families connected and provide support during crises, currently has users in more than twenty-eight countries. Our family will never be the same, yet we are closer, stronger, and more aware of one another's needs by sharing our grief. I think Justin would be proud of us for continuing his legacy in a way that helps people and potentially saves lives.

My journey has underscored the transformative strength of self-belief, proving that even in the face of profound personal loss and daunting challenges, the power to achieve remarkable milestones lies within each of us. By embracing our innate resilience and refusing to underestimate our capabilities, we can transcend adversity and realize our most audacious dreams. I encourage you to dream big dreams and develop yourself in a way that's authentic to you, too—something that paves the way to your ultimate fulfillment.

Karen Osborne, founder of Karen Renee Interior Design, has more than thirty years of experience in merchandising model homes. An NCIDQ-certified professional, she mentors emerging designers and has served on the Maryland ASID (American Society of Interior Designers) board for many years. Karen's passion lies in creating model homes that resonate with buyers, transforming their dreams into reality. She is a trusted asset to home builders, known for her attentive and innovative talent. Additionally, Karen has assisted with high school leadership programs and has dedicated numerous years to supporting nonprofits in the fields of mental health, healthcare, and domestic violence.

karenreneeinteriors.com

LISTENING FOR BEAUTY

Nadia Rahali

Truth, and goodness, and beauty are but different faces of the same all.
—Ralph Waldo Emerson

As a teenager, I often found our home in Casablanca unbearably monotonous. The quiet neighborhood, with its well-manicured front yards, neatly trimmed hedges, and beautiful cascading bright magenta bougainvillea on the villa walls, felt like a shipping container suffocating my free-spirited nature. The predictable routines only heightened my sense of confinement.

One day, after an argument with my mother, my desire for independence and insatiable curiosity drove me to plot an escape to the nearby shantytown, where our nanny's family lived. While my mother napped and my younger siblings played with the water hose in the garden, I packed a small bag and slipped out through the heavy gate of our home.

The journey took me about two hours, and as I approached the shantytown, I was struck by its vibrant atmosphere. A labyrinth of mud roads, makeshift homes of corrugated metal and wood, and the sounds of Moroccan folk music created a stark contrast to the silence of my home. The shantytown was teeming with life, far removed from the quiet, middle-class world I knew.

I quickly made friends with the locals, who were curious about this young girl who had left the comfort of her middle-class home. They welcomed me warmly, sharing their stories, food, and lives. We danced to lively music, shared meals cooked with love, fetched water together, and laughed over tales of their experiences. Despite the hardships they faced, there was an undeniable joy in their way of life—a resilience and a strong sense of community that deeply inspired me.

After three days with our nanny's family, my father came to take me back home. Living in the shantytown wasn't easy; the days were hot, and the nights were cold. But every moment was filled with the richness of real experience. I learned to appreciate simple pleasures—a shared meal, a kind word, a moment of connection. The people I met taught me that joy could be found even in the most unexpected places and that seeking it was a journey worth taking. I discovered at a young age that the world was full of beauty, even in the most humble and challenging places.

Years later, I found myself in an abusive marriage. The vibrant, free-spirited girl who once roamed the shantytowns of Casablanca felt trapped again, but this time by a different kind ofconfinement. The emotional, physical, and psychological strain was overwhelming. As an immigrant without family nearby, the situation felt even more isolating and dangerous.

To cope, I poured all my energy and heart into my work. It became my refuge, the only place where I could express myself and find a sense of purpose. One day, my manager called me into his office and said, "Nadia, come with me to this event in the cafeteria at 2:00 p.m." It was an introduction to the United Way and the work they do in the community. The spokesperson shared how they help people in need, and I was especially interested when she mentioned their support for women who are victims of domestic violence.

After the talk, my manager turned to me and said, "Nadia, you should contribute to this organization."

I looked at him, saddened, and said, "I don't make enough money to give."

He replied, "Nadia, it's not the amount that matters; it's the act of giving that counts."

His words inspired me, and I contributed to the United Way. That simple act made me see myself differently; I started to see myself as someone who could make a difference.

One day, after a particularly big fight with my husband, I felt overwhelmed and desperate. When he left the house, I called the United Way 211 hotline and spoke to a social worker. She referred me to a shelter for battered women. Drawing on the courage I had as a teenager, I packed my clothes and books and left. I headed to Atlanta, seeking a new beginning and a promise of safety and hope.

I declared that I wanted to be of service—to give back and be someone who makes a difference. As I searched for work, I stumbled upon a position with the United Way, the same organization that had once saved my life. I felt a deep sense of guidance and believed this opportunity was a creation of my own making. It turned out that the role I was applying for—an account manager for a new community center that convened civic and philanthropic communities—had been open for six months as they struggled to find the perfect fit.

I applied and soon received a call for an interview. As I emerged from the bustling Five Points train station in downtown Atlanta, I was reminded of my adventurous days in Casablanca. I felt a mix of fear, timidity, excitement, and anticipation, eager to discover what lay ahead for me.

During the interview, the chief financial officer decided to see if the CEO was available to meet. I nervously walked down a beautiful modern staircase to the CEO's office. After a brief conversation, he looked at me and said, "You are the one we have been waiting for." I was hired on the spot.

As an account manager, I focused on building relationships and fostering a sense of community. Over time, I rose to the position of director, helping to establish the Loudermilk Center as a key institution in Atlanta.

Even in my darkest moments, I held on to the lessons I had learned in the shantytown. The resilience of the people there, their ability to find joy in the simplest things, and the strength of community—even if it was just within myself—gave me hope. I knew that, just as I had once found beauty and joy in unexpected places, I could find the strength to rebuild and reclaim my life.

My journey was far from easy, but it constantly reminded me that there is always a way forward, even in the most challenging times. The courageous young girl who had escaped to the shantytown remained within me, guiding me through my experiences as an immigrant. She helped me seek out a better life, make a difference, contribute, and be of service.

Nadia Rahali is the director of The Loudermilk Center, a nationally recognized institution driving meaningful change through civic engagement, nonprofit collaboration, and philanthropic initiatives. With years of experience in convening diverse stakeholders, Nadia has been instrumental in elevating the Center's impact on communities across the country. She is also the founder of *Movere Alliance*, a niche consulting firm dedicated to helping non-profit leaders unlock their full potential. Nadia holds a degree in Political Science and African American Studies from Old Dominion University and has furthered her expertise with a certification in Sustainability Strategies for Industries from MIT.

moverealliance.com

ROOTS OF PASSION

Sandy Rasch

People often ask me about my path to becoming an artist. Specifically, they wonder how I made the transition from corporate life to a daily life of creativity. To arrive at the answer, I took a self-reflective journey. This self-exam helped me understand where my passion and creativity are rooted. It also strengthened my appreciation for the lessons in each of my life experiences. I could have come no other way.

The process also helped me realize that my attention to detail is part of having interest, love, and compassion for the people around me. It is also the basis for self-love and self-compassion. Creativity, regardless of the form it takes, is an active sharing of that interest, love, and compassion. We do not create in a vacuum. Creativity is a natural unfolding of expression in beautiful upward spiral. It is a perpetual transformation that keeps us moving and trying new expressions. There is no set timeline for expression—only that it must take place.

I like to claim that I have not changed much since early childhood, and perhaps in many ways, that may be observed today. I was a very weird kid.

I grew up on the Mississippi Gulf Coast, so I was afforded the opportunity to be a saltwater kid who trailered a boat before I had a driver's license. I always felt a part of nature. I loved rainy days and surf. I learned later that I was enjoying the negative ions in the air. I would lie in our gravel driveway with the dogs and stir the dust with the breath from my nose, as they did. I enjoyed that experience of peace and connection. I would imagine traveling into the earth following the roots of the giant oak trees in our yard. Many years later, I read that this is a shamanic practice to connect with earth and with spirit guides. Though my actions—and indeed my weirdness—may have appeared whacky to some and random to others, they were designed to satisfy my deep requirements for connection, joy, and passion.

Woodwork and painting, like yard work, require raw material, a blank canvas or some other well-defined starting point, and a commitment to the task. It is very rewarding to start with one thing, work on it for some hours, and end with a profoundly different result. I found many opportunities to be able to meet my strong appetite for immediate gratification.

Considering my deeply rooted operating strategies, the evolution from design engineer to artist may appear to be direct and natural. From a different perspective, it may also be seen as a devolution, a return to childhood thrills. I have always gravitated to activities that satisfy the part of me that loves a clean sheet of paper and a sharp pencil.

I have early, vivid core memories of being full of pure joy and excitement. These inspiring episodes were associated with simple objects like new school supplies and with activities like following the plans to build a model. A retrospective look at my early jobs, education, and life experiences reflects my internal gravitation to fun. I could always find that joy and passion, even in the most unlikely settings.

I enlisted in the United States Navy out of high school rather than starting college. It makes sense now that it would have been my opinion that college was an important opportunity only for serious students and that I would know myself well enough to realize I should do some growing up before undertaking higher education. I studied electronics and communications and became a second class petty officer (ET2). The big personal takeaway for me from that experience was that I need to know where my couch is, and that it will not be moved unless I plan to move it. We can add controlling to weird.

I worked as a broadcast engineer for a several years in the pre-IP (internet protocol) era. At that time, television and radio were provided solely over radio frequency, requiring remote operation of the huge transmitters. I switched on air, performed many production-assistant roles, and engineered remote transmissions. The sights and sounds of the studio, the lights, the cameras, the microphones were all very familiar to me because I had been in the studio as a child. My father was a producer and engineer of both television and radio. He was also the local weatherman when I was very small. These experiences shaped my creativity and what I believed possible.

I did go to college ten years after high school to earn a BS in mathematics. Evidently, I was continuing to build my weirdness and nerdiness. I had two unique goals as an undergrad: to demonstrate to my kids that they could undertake any goal successfully at any time they wish, and to have my beloved grandmother see me walk across the stage to receive my diploma.

Graduate school offered me the chance to intern with a world-renowned physicist. I was given a project to order the materials and fabricate a shielded container for the uranium we used in the lab. Though this was a very small part of an enormous research project, this experience forever elevated the way I viewed my value. Being given this level of trust and responsibility created a deep sense of accomplishment. My creativity and passion are connected to that sense. Each feeds the other in profound ways. I went on the earn an MS in environmental management and an MA in telecommunications.

I was hired as a statistical analyst by the Houston Police Department, made possible by the referral of a dear friend. Early on, I was asked to organize a large pile of mail and invoices. I took care of that assignment and prepared the bills for the captain's signature. Later that day, the pile reappeared on my desk with sticky notes on many pages indicating that the signature of the division budget coordinator was required. I asked my sergeant where to direct the pile for signatures. She replied, "That's you. Sign them and send them out." Soon I was promoted to Administrative Assistant II. This would not be the first time that performance preceded promotion.

The first day on the job as communications design engineer, I sat in my large office and marveled at the desk, the drafting table, and the design tools put there for my use. I was giddy with excitement, inspiration, and confidence. I've always taken great satisfaction in problem solving. Putting things on paper and understanding diagrams still thrill me today.

For several years, I worked remotely with clients all over the world. Working from home required me to create a balance of work and recreational activity. I had an easel in my home office. It felt natural to simply spin my chair around and trade my computer screen and keyboard for a canvas and brush. I filled the canvas many times with therapeutic strokes only to paint the entire thing white for a fresh start. This multilayered canvas is the first one that I ever sold. I was asked to provide a number of works to help fill a wall in a Houston art exhibit. One of the artists was unable to participate, leaving an unsavory blank space. I obliged and quickly learned there is a buyer for every piece. What a great lesson in value!

Today, my art pieces are often inspired by the energy around me. Materials have energy, history, and frequency that often tell me what the creative expression will be. This is a subtle but remarkable difference between art and the world of corporate responsibility. I enjoy a good plan for creating art, but now I am quick to change a plan to follow the flow of energy at any given time.

I have been granted Artist Certification by the Museum of the Americas. I have participated in exhibitions in Dubai, UAE; Madrid, Spain; and Houston, Texas. My desire is that my art pieces offer every individual a moment of what he or she needs, whether wonder, pleasure, distraction, or inspiration.

What childhood memory can you connect with that makes you smile? What early object, person, or circumstance inspires peace or power or joy for you? Find this core memory, and you may find a well of personal strength. Use it to bring clarity to current projects. Feed it. It is standing by to feed you. These early joyful moments of play may be the basis for new inspiration and passion.

Sandy Rasch's appreciation of art and design began in childhood and continues to expand. Since 2018, she has been enjoying retirement from a thirty-year career in the electronics and communications industries. She now uses her time and talent to develop unique art pieces in wood, clay, and on canvas. Her work can be found on display and in private collections around the world. Sandy's greatest inspiration comes from nature. Many of her unique pieces are created from natural and found materials and are influenced by ecology and sustainability. Sandy desires the inspiration of the creative process to be seen and felt in each piece.

sandyleafdesigns.com

BEYOND THE STORM: MY PATH TO EMBRACING AND CONQUERING LIFE'S CHALLENGES

Carolyn Ross

I would like to give you a glimpse into what being *unstoppable* has meant for me. At the age of fifteen, I became pregnant. My first thought was suicide due to the shame and embarrassment I endured from having to tell my parents and having to go to school pregnant. I hid it for three months until my father confronted me and made me tell him who the father was and where he lived. No one would have ever thought that one of the smartest and quietest girls in the school would become pregnant. This begins my story of being unstoppable.

As a teenage girl, I came a broken home and was raised in a small American town where most folks worked picking fruit in the form of oranges, grapefruits, tomatoes, and green bell peppers. With this teenage pregnancy, this was my perceived existence. However, I made the decision that neither I nor my unborn child would be a statistic.

I had no idea what all of that meant at my young age, but I knew it would be difficult.

When I was sixteen and in eleventh grade, I gave birth to a five pound, five ounce baby boy. I graduated high school, but prior to that, I had taken the ASVAB (Armed Forces Vocational Aptitude Test). I did it just to get out of a class, not knowing it would alter the course of my life. I initially wanted to go to college, get a degree, and become a lawyer, but now those plans for higher education were delayed. Instead, I was pregnant and raising a baby on my own; there was no child support or involvement from the child's father. I had no idea how I was going to make it in this world with a small child and no financial support. My mother bore the financial burden of taking care of me and my son while I continued on in school.

During my senior year, an older girl from my neighborhood had gone into the military and came to our high school to discuss the benefits of military service and encourage high schoolers to join the army. She was wearing her uniform, smiling, and looking sharp. When I saw her, something clicked in my head, and I told myself this was my ticket out of small-town America.

I didn't tell my mother or father right away. I first spoke to the recruiter, and he came to our home since I was not old enough at that time to enter into a contract and my mother's permission and signature were needed. She also agreed to take custody of my young son. I enlisted in the military, left home, and my journey of being unstoppable continued.

When I left active duty, I enlisted in the army reserve, but I was lost, confused, and depressed after leaving active-duty military service. There were no transition services available, and there was no one I could to turn to for help. I had one setback after another over the next ten years of my military career. I was in a very toxic and abusive relationship for five years. When I ended that relationship, it changed the trajectory of my life personally and professionally for the better. I came to my senses, regained my confidence, and decided to join the Florida Army National Guard to finish up my career and work toward retirement.

Next, I pursued my dream of going to college and finishing my degree, which I had started while on active duty. By this time, I had another child, and it was very challenging to finish school, work full-time, and raise two children alone. It took me seven years to get my associate degree. I spent many evenings prior to going to class crying in my car because I was so tired and didn't want to go to class. My goal was to graduate with honors, and I did that—but barely. The stress of raising children, working, and all the other things necessary to move my life forward was overwhelming. At this point, I had placed my vision of going to law school on pause until I figured out what I wanted to do with my life post-active duty military.

During this time, by chance I applied for a role at a call center. The recruiter just happened to be a member of my church, and he started talking to me about his role and what he was doing. He was also was a military veteran and was attending Saint Leo University, MacDill Air Force Base to get an HR degree. I felt that this was something that I could do, something that fit my personality, and I decided to pursue a career in human resources as well.

I enrolled in Saint Leo and began the journey to get my bachelor's degree in human resources management. The program was an eight-week accelerated course, which was challenging. I went to school full-time at night as well as on the weekends, and it all paid off—I eventually graduated with honors.

By the time I finished my bachelor's degree, I finally had received acceptance back into the Florida Army National Guard after a yearlong battle to prove I would be an asset to the organization. I missed the military and longed to be a part of it again.

The next phase of my life came when I deployed to Iraq and had to leave my preteen son with his father, who was unprepared for the responsibility of being a full-time parent. It was tough being in a war environment not knowing if I would come home with all my limbs or come home in a body bag. The stress of this was overwhelming, and I was not treated well by some my fellow soldiers in arms, which only made the experience even worse.

I returned home after eighteen months of active duty, one year of it in Iraq and Kuwait. I faced another difficult adjustment—my son had grown up while I was gone; he had become very self-sufficient and really didn't need me much.

I still didn't really know what I wanted to do or where I belonged. The unstoppable me felt stifled professionally and personally. I made the decision to leave a very large company and instead accepted a role with a small company. I then decided it was time for me to take another leap and work on my master's degree. By hindsight, I realize that I jumped from the frying pan into the fire a mere two months after returning from deployment. I failed to give myself time to decompress and came close to having a nervous breakdown. The program was accelerated, but I did it and graduated with honors.

I'm sharing my story because while it wasn't an easy journey, I never gave up. I chose to be unstoppable There were so many peaks and valleys, and at times, all I wanted to do was stay in bed, crawl under my covers, and hide. There was so much stigma that came with coming from a broken home, experiencing a teen pregnancy, being an unwed mother, and it would have been easy for me to just cave in to all of it and be one more statistic. But instead, over and over again, I chose to be resilient, pursue new challenges and opportunities, and do whatever it took to be a success and create a meaningful life. If I can encourage one woman not to give up, then telling my story will be worth it. I want everyone to know that with perseverance, patience, and hard work, it's possible to realize your dreams. You, too, can be unstoppable!

Carolyn Ross is an accomplished HR professional specializing in employee relations with extensive experience and a proven track record in conflict resolution and fostering positive workplace environments. A proud army veteran who served her country with distinction, including a deployment to Iraq during a wartime conflict, she brings a disciplined and strategic approach to her work. Outside of her professional life, Carolyn is dedicated to volunteering for veterans' organizations and initiatives supporting low-income women and children. Her commitment to service, both professionally and personally, underscores her passion for helping others and making a meaningful impact.

linkedin.com/in/carolynross2

FROM IMPOSTER TO UNSTOPPABLE

Stacey Ruth

D on't let anyone tell you that being a woman in business is no different than being a man in business. They either have no idea what they are talking about, or they are lying to you. This reality hit me hard in the early 2000s when I found myself broken down, both physically and emotionally, on my office restroom floor. In that moment of vulnerability, I confronted the harsh truth: I had betrayed my own body and values in a relentless pursuit of a flawed version of perfection, one dictated by societal standards not aligned with my authenticity.

This realization marked my awakening to the debilitating effects of imposter syndrome—a condition that disproportionately affects women and high achievers. I had been chasing societal markers of success— degrees, income, recognition—all the while feeling like an imposter in my own life. This disconnect between my external accomplishments and internal sense of self was the source of my profound discomfort. However, this bottom I was hitting was also the beginning of something truly miraculous. As popular psychologist Adam Grant posted on LinkedIn, imposter syndrome "is not a clue you are unqualified. It's a sign of hidden potential." Of course, sitting on the restroom floor, I could not have heard or understood any of that. I was in freefall, like Icarus flying too close to the sun. My hidden potential was to be my full, unapologetic, and unstoppable self. Ironically, that was the very thing I felt least qualified to be.

When I founded my first agency in the late 1990s, I entered a daunting world of live corporate events that was mostly a man's domain—aggressive, highly competitive, stress-charged, dismissive, and unforgiving. I was a fledgling entrepreneur with no business or leadership experience trying to carve out a space for myself.

At that time, resources that are readily available today—networking groups, niche industry associations, and mentors—were scarce. I had a few business books and role models from previous jobs, but often, I found myself mimicking behaviors that did not align with my intrinsic style. I was performing the role of a confident, seasoned entrepreneur, masking my internal feelings of inadequacy and the constant fear of being exposed as a fraud—too young, too inexperienced, and too female to thrive among the sharks.

My journey was riddled with missteps that were both humbling and costly, which only seemed to prove I was out of my league. In the chaotic juggle of entrepreneurship, I once lost a thirty-thousand dollar check by distractedly leaving it on the roof of my car as I drove away. Another time, overwhelmed by my responsibilities and unschooled in effective delegation with oversight, I turned over every single component of my bookkeeping to a seemingly qualified office manager who then stole my identity. These experiences painfully underscored the need for a fundamental change in how I managed my focus and energy.

To bolster my confidence, I surrounded myself with less-experienced staff and even ceded significant ownership to two male partners, inadvertently undermining my own position and authority. This setup left me in a perpetual state of defense, always reacting rather than leading strategically. My partners scrutinized every decision, and I found myself unable to step back and guide my team from a place of strength and creativity.

I found myself constantly disempowered and off balance despite my current CEO role and my long history as a high achiever—from being a straight-A student and National Merit Finalist to earning a full scholarship and graduating with honors. However, it was not unfamiliar for me to feel like an outsider. In college, during a theoretical mathematics class with only two women, my professor blatantly told the class that women did not belong in mathematics.

The implicit and explicit messages from my professor, my industry, and society as a whole, telling me I didn't belong, were planted in my brain in a way I didn't truly recognize.

I didn't let it stop me, of course. I was named among the top 50 Entrepreneurs under 50 in Atlanta, and my agency was twice named one of the top one hundred "it" agencies in the country. Except I was working twice as hard as anyone else to get there, which came at an extraordinary cost—to myself, my health, my relationships, and to my team. The relentless pursuit of traditional success took a severe toll on my personal life and health. My agency suffered from high turnover; I went through two marriages; and I was perpetually exhausted. The pressure to conform to a masculine model of business leadership, emphasizing relentless competition and constant visibility, clashed with my inherent style, which leaned toward collaboration, empathy, and empowerment.

As a high-achieving woman, and also as an entrepreneur, I was just embodying what the statistics predict. Today, more than 70 percent of adults admit to feeling they are hiding their authentic selves at work. The majority of those self-reporting this inner attitude are either women, entrepreneurs, or both. This statistic also affects underrepresented demographics everywhere. We are the ones who look around and see no one like us. We are first, only, and different. We're afraid of not being enough in some way or feeling like we are undeserving of our achievements, and therefore are a fraud.

Living like this, a crash is bound to happen. We can only hope our wakeup call shakes us out of the illusion that we are mandated to live our lives and run our businesses like somebody else. We aren't.

Once I literally picked myself up off the floor, I began a long, gradual process to uncover and activate my own innate leadership and entrepreneurial style. It took me nearly two decades to feel I had unlearned all the old lessons society had taught me. But, like my entrepreneurial journey, I was forging my own path. I look around today and see I was not alone in my efforts. Hundreds—maybe even thousands—of women are recognizing that not only do we lead and run companies differently, it's also necessary to have diverse styles for sustainability.

I founded Unstoppable Leader and Her CEO Life to help women just like me to build personal brands and thought leadership for themselves in the most authentic, clear, confident way possible. As a survivor of the hard-hitting masculine approach to business, I define *unstoppable* as a fluid and dynamic experience, more like water than a jack hammer. When I am unstoppable, I meet life's obstacles by flowing around them or over them, then returning to my inevitable course.

I learned to do this by getting unwavering clarity about my values, which oddly enough are not about being powerful, but about being empowering. They're not about competing, but about collaborating. They are not about doing, but about being.

I also leaned into meditation and asking myself powerful self-coaching questions daily, such as: "What intention do I want to bring to my day today?" or "Where is it time for me to grow and take a risk?" This was the inspiration for starting Her CEO Life, where women founders can collaborate with one another and still the noise of those voices that tell us we aren't doing it right.

Most importantly, I had internalized the voices, like that old professor who told me I didn't belong and wasn't enough. It's so difficult to distance ourselves from that inner critic. We tend automatically to believe everything we think, despite all evidence to the contrary! Meditation and affirmations retrained my brain over time. Where once that voice was subtly telling me things like:

- I'm not smart enough.
- I'm not experienced enough.
- I will fail.
- I am flawed.
- No one wants to pay that much for my work.
- This is the best I can expect.
- No one wants to hear what I have to say.

I rescripted alternative affirmations:

- I am highly intelligent and can find a solution.
- I have a lifetime of experience I can bring to this situation.
- I have a unique perspective that deserves to be shared.

As I share my journey, my hope is to inspire other women to recognize and challenge the insidious effects of imposter syndrome that may be holding them back. We are not bound to live our lives or run our businesses according to someone else's blueprint. We are capable of defining and achieving success on our own terms, and in doing so, we not only fulfill our potential but also pave the way for others to follow.

By advocating for authenticity and resilience, I have become not just a participant in my industry but a leader shaping its future. My story, from imposter to unstoppable, underscores that the greatest challenges we face can lead to our most significant transformations, fostering a leadership style that is not only effective but also is true to who we are.

Stacey Ruth is the founder and CEO of Her CEO Life, a female founders community, and The Unstoppable Leader, a leadership development and personal branding firm. She has founded two multimillion-dollar agencies, has been among the Top 50 Entrepreneurs Under 50 in Atlanta, and twice awarded Top 100 "It" Agencies by Experiential Marketer. Today Stacey helps other women leaders bust through society's limiting messages so they can truly be unstoppable in their most authentic self. Her books, *Own Your Own Shift*, *Inside Out Smart*, and *Branded for Impact* are available now at Amazon and Barnes & Noble.

unstoppable-leader.com

HELP FROM HIGH PLACES

Gretchen M. Stein, PhD

When I was invited to write a chapter in this book, I saw it as an opportunity to share the secrets to my success that I believe are available to anyone. I am saying things here that come from my life experiences, things I have never shared before.

In my late twenties, I went through a period of extreme loss that was life-transforming. One tragic Thanksgiving, my father left the table surrounded by his family and went off for the last canoe ride of the season. He never returned. A few years later, my mother literally died of a broken heart while undergoing sextuple bypass surgery. During this period, I also experienced the loss of a lifelong dream—the dream of a happy marriage and family that dissolved when my grade school sweetheart and I divorced.

Many people grow stronger in their spiritual beliefs during difficult times. I did too. Perhaps because I no longer had two parents or a husband to discuss things with, I turned inward for divine guidance. I began to meditate, pray more, and simply sit in silence. I found that still small voice within. My belief in God increased exponentially.

At this time, I was the chief operating officer for a family service organization, leading the division that offered employee assistance programs (EAP). Twenty-four hours a day, seven days a week, our division marketed and provided professional counseling, workplace training, and supervisor consulting services to employers to help their employees deal with life problems that if left unaddressed would cause productivity problems at work.

It was at this job that I met Joan Sirotiak. I believe that every person you meet has the power to potentially change the rest of your life. This truth became reality for us both when Joan came for a job interview. Fifteen minutes into the interview, I had an inner knowing that Joan and I would make a great work team. Little did we know then how our lives would interweave over the next thirty-three years.

I knew I needed to dream new dreams for my life and for the lives of my young children. I began to think about what I really wanted to be, do, and create with my life. The seed of an idea of going out on my own and creating a better version of what I was doing began to develop and grow into a strong desire in my heart that reflected my soul's purpose. I asked Joan if she would like to join me. She did.

We were two single women in our thirties. Our greatest strength came from a power you could not see in our resumes. We are deeply spiritual, prayerful women. Our courage to step out of our comfortable, well-paying jobs to go out on our own was a giant leap of faith; faith in ourselves, faith in each other, and faith in God. We learned to befriend our fears and go forward. We promised this dream would not only bring us to the place we needed to be but would also bring much good for others.

In 1994, we took our strong faith over fear, our powerful intuition, and my home equity along with my kids' college funds as loan collateral and started the Sand Creek Group. This became a 100 percent women-owned business that we co-created with Spirit out of our natural strengths as women.

Once we made a total commitment to our dream, all manner of miracles occurred. Two previously unknown revenue streams showed up. Our dream office on a scenic river became available to us, even though originally a larger company had signed a multiyear lease on that space. It was a constant reminder to "go with the flow." Throughout the many years we ran this company, the perfect employee for the right job would show up at our door at the right time. Our customers also came to us in similar ways.

Marianne Williamson in her *Meditations for a Miraculous Life* says, "The key to power when it comes to your work life is to remember you are there in the service of God." For twenty-five years, the Sand Creek Group operated under a big, bold mission of providing love and service to all. Love, in the business world in which we operated, translated as care, compassion, kindness, and generosity.

I enjoy telling this story because it speaks of the miracles that surrounded us and exposes the secret to our success that came as Spirit-led guidance through dreams, gut-level hunches, out-of-the-blue thoughts, and divine ideas. We moved beyond our five senses into knowing and tapped into this additional intelligence system. As I have told many people I have mentored over the years, "Develop your intuition, listen to your intuition, and trust your intuition."

The great miracle that skyrocketed our new start-up business to early success started with an extraordinary dream Joan had. In it, I was shaking the hand of then President Clinton. He was thanking me. I acknowledged the dream as significant, but I did not yet know what it foretold.

However, three days later in the *Commerce Business Daily*, the purchasing publication for the federal government, the Executive Office of the President of the United States (EOP) was requesting proposals for an employee assistance program, the very thing our new business was selling. Because we were a brand-new company and this was a request for services from the highest level of the federal government, many would have dismissed this opportunity as an impossibility. Joan's dream and our trust in our guidance, however, gave us the courage to try. We put together the best proposal we could, sent it off with our prayers and a tiny angel riding in the envelope. Two months later, it was our office grand opening, and Joan took the call from the EOP. The caller asked, "Could Dr. Stein be in Washington, DC, on Monday?"

Joan immediately said "yes," as there was no need to check the calendar for this request!

I flew to Washington, DC, to present our services on the very week the doors of our company officially opened! Upon arrival, I went through security and was told which floor to go to, but I wasn't given a room number. When I exited the elevator, no one was there to meet me. I waited and then ducked into the ladies' restroom for a conversation with God.

Already overwhelmed by the whole experience, I said to the mirror, "OK, God, this deal is way bigger than I am; you will have to take it from here." And that's exactly what happened. I surrendered it all to the Source of all and God took it from there. When I walked out of the ladies' room, a woman met me and escorted me to an impressive conference room. Managers from seventeen agencies within the EOP were waiting to interview me.

The woman at the head of the table greeted me by saying, "You women from Minnesota always have the most beautiful winter coats." It was a very kind way of helping me to relax in this high-powered room.

I responded, "Oh, do you know women from Minnesota?" It turned out the two women running this meeting had lived in Minnesota, and one's mother still did.

With that, I felt connected, and I surrendered. I fell into the zone and relaxed into the chair with words flowing from me, but not of me, for the next two hours. At the conclusion, I literally floated out and onto Pennsylvania Ave. We soon learned that Sand Creek had been awarded the contract to provide counseling, training, and consultation to all employees and their family members of the EOP, including the White House staff. Not only for that contract period but for many more years to come, as we served through historically significant times in the Clinton, Bush, Obama, and Trump presidencies.

Over the years, we built our dream from an idea to a company that provided loving, compassionate service to hundreds of thousands of employees and their family members in the United States, Central America, Europe, and Asia. We worked with an amazing variety of workplaces, including many federal and county government agencies, the Office of the Commissioner of Major League Baseball, eight MLB clubs, other professional sports organizations, Fortune 500 companies, and healthcare systems.

Sand Creek not only grew by reputation and sales but also by acquisition. Three of our competitors sold their companies to us when they retired. One said to me, "I would only sell my company to you." We even purchased the organization where Joan and I first met. We had come full circle.

In 2019, Joan and I sold our company and retired from EAP work. Today, I continue to live my mission of love and service as a Dream Builder Life Coach, helping others to manifest big dreams and live the life they would love to live.

What is inside you is far greater than any challenges you are facing. This quote from Goethe inspires me to action: "Whatever you can do or dream you can, begin it. Boldness has genius, power, and magic in it." Today is your moment. Today is YOUR day to take bold action.

Gretchen M. Stein, PhD, is the co-founder of the Sand Creek Group Ltd., an international corporation specializing in organization development and employee assistance programs. From 1994–2019, she served as president and CEO. A popular speaker, writer, psychotherapist, and highly respected organization consultant, Gretchen holds a doctorate from the College of Education and Human Development at the University of Minnesota, where she was honored with the Award of Distinguished Alumni for bringing distinction to her profession and for her significant contributions to behavioral healthcare delivery and leadership. She is certified as a life coach with the Brave Thinking Institute. Gretchen is a lifelong member of Rotary International.

gretchenmstein.com

THE POWER OF RELATIONSHIPS: MY PATH TO REBUILDING

Dr. Tashana Thompson

There I was, a heap of snot and tears, crying my heart out to my husband, Brian, at lunch at a local tavern. I was careful to muffle my tears so the other patrons didn't know the truth about me. I was failing, broke, miserable, and not sure that I could go on. The absolute despair on my husband's face was palpable. Here I was, his strong woman, his wife, and the mother of his baby girl, falling apart because I was battling nearly debilitating postpartum depression, financial ruin, and the abandonment of my business partner and close friend.

We welcomed our daughter, Addisyn, on January 11, 2017, and the months that followed nearly killed me. In fact, I'm sure I died a thousand tiny deaths during that period. I was miserable at home, balancing being a new wife and mother with being a stepmom to Brian's son, Isaac, from his previous marriage. Our relationship was filled with love but also the complexities that come with blended families. In less than a year, I had gone from being a vibrant business owner earning six figures to bankruptcy court just one month after my daughter's birth because I literally could not pay my bills. The loss of one very large client had pulled the rug from under my business and life as I knew it. Now, here I was, having suicidal ideations while pumping milk for my brand-new baby.

This summer day, I couldn't take anymore: My business partner and dearest friend, a woman who, over the last decade of doing business together, had become like a sister to me, had abandoned me. She left the business in May to save herself from the financial ruin we were experiencing, and Lord, I couldn't blame her. There wasn't enough money to support both of us.

At that lunch, the tears and devastation became my manifestation and a vow I made to myself, God, and my tiny baby girl that I was going to do better for us—better for myself. I made a vow that I would rebuild myself, my business, and my brand. How would I do it? By doing what I love with people I adored who valued the unique branding and marketing expertise I bring to the world. I call these people my soulmate clients, and I was on a quest to find them and to nurture the relationships with the amazing women who were already in my circle.

The journey was anything but easy. I understood that rebuilding my business and life wasn't just about money. I had to do some real soul work. For me, this included returning to the roots of my faith. Prayer and meditation became like oxygen to me, and it literally has fueled every decision I've made since that point. I began carving out time for me and my Creator; spending time with God was literally the key to it all.

From there, I was able to focus on the business, which included joining a networking group specifically focused on bringing together women in business. I was intentional about surrounding myself with people who believed in me even when I couldn't believe in myself. The women from my networking group became a lifeline for my business, offering tons of introductions and ultimately, business. Their support was invaluable, and I began to see a glimmer of hope.

One of the first people to support me was my longtime client Vicki. She not only believed in my vision but also referred business my way and did plenty of work with me that helped me to keep contributing to my household. Helping me rebuild from the ground up, her unwavering support was a beacon of light during my darkest days.

I had the pleasure of working with an amazing woman who was my first client after having Addisyn. She trusted me with her business, and that trust reignited my passion for what I did. Working with her reminded me of why I started my business in the first place.

To make it all work, I needed help outside of my home and business. I needed care that I could trust for Addisyn. Ms. Monique, a kind and nurturing woman, babysat Addisyn while I worked. Her presence allowed me to focus on rebuilding my business, knowing my daughter was in good hands.

Finally, there was my first love, my mom, Tonya, who was my prayer warrior and live-in support while Brian worked nights. She not only provided emotional support but also contributed financially, keeping the mortgage paid and food on the table. Her sacrifices and prayers were my backbone then and still are to this day.

I redefined my business, focusing on what I loved and what I was truly passionate about. I sought out my soulmate clients, those who valued my unique branding and marketing expertise. Slowly but surely, I began to rebuild my brand.

Relationship Marketing: Building Bonds Beyond Business

Relationship marketing became the cornerstone of my strategy. I focused on building genuine connections with my clients, understanding their needs, and providing tailored solutions. This approach not only helped me retain clients but also generated referrals, creating a ripple effect of growth. Relationship marketing isn't just about transactions; it's about transforming clients into loyal advocates.

By investing time in getting to know my clients on a personal level, I was able to create customized experiences that resonated with them. I hosted client appreciation events, sent personalized thank-you notes, and regularly checked in with them, not just for business purposes but also to see how they were doing in their lives. This personal touch fostered a sense of trust and loyalty that went beyond the typical client-service provider dynamic.

I also leveraged social media to maintain these connections, sharing not only business updates but also personal milestones and stories. This transparency and authenticity allowed clients to see me as more than just a business owner—they saw me as a person who genuinely cared about their success and well-being.

Through relationship marketing, I created a community of like-minded individuals who supported one another. Clients began referring me to their friends and colleagues, and soon, my network expanded exponentially. The positive word-of-mouth exposure generated from these genuine relationships became a powerful marketing tool that no amount of advertising could replicate.

The first year was a struggle. There were days when I wanted to give up, when the weight of my past failures threatened to crush me. But I kept pushing forward, driven by the promise I had made to Addisyn and to myself.

By the second year, things started to turn around. My client base grew, and with it, my confidence. I nurtured relationships with the amazing women in my circle, drawing strength from their support and encouragement.

When the pandemic hit, I saw an opportunity to build community in a new way. I started hosting a virtual event called "Coffee with Tashana." It became a space where I could share my unique perspective on branding and marketing with an online audience. This initiative not only helped me stay connected with my clients but also expanded my reach, bringing in new clients who resonated with my message and approach.

Five years later, my business was thriving. I had gone from earning $24K in 2017 to $500K! It was a testament to the power of resilience, determination, and the unwavering belief that I could create a better future.

As I sat in my home office, looking out at the beautiful trees in my front yard, I felt a sense of peace that had eluded me for so long. Addisyn's laughter echoed throughout the house, a reminder of the joy that had come from the darkest days of my life.

Brian walked in, a smile on his face. "You did it, Shana, you really did it."

I turned to him, my heart swelling with gratitude. "We did it," I corrected. "I couldn't have done it without you."

He wrapped his arms around me, and for the first time in years, I felt whole. The journey had been long and arduous, but it had led me to a place of strength and fulfillment. I had rebuilt my life, not just for myself but for my family. In doing so, I discovered a resilience I never knew I had.

The future was bright, filled with endless possibilities. As I looked at my family, I knew that no matter what challenges lay ahead, we would face them together. In the end, it wasn't just about rebuilding a business; it was about reclaiming my life and finding the strength to rise from the ashes.

As you navigate your own challenges and setbacks, remember that within you lies an incredible strength waiting to be discovered. Embrace each obstacle as an opportunity for growth, knowing that your journey is uniquely yours. Never underestimate the power of relationships in your life and business. As I often say, "Our lives and businesses run at the speed of our relationships." The connections we forge, nurture, and maintain can be the lifeline that pulls us through our darkest moments and propels us toward success.

Surround yourself with those who believe in you, support your dreams, and inspire you to be your best self. These relationships will not only help you weather the storms but also celebrate your triumphs as you rebuild and thrive.

Dr. Tashana Thompson is a seasoned chief marketing officer with more than twenty years of experience in branding, marketing, and visibility strategy. She holds dual master's degrees in marketing and human resources and a doctorate in Christian leadership and business. As the CEO of Beyond Business Solutions, she provides holistic support to small businesses, helping them thrive through custom strategies. Known for her warmth, relatability, and professionalism, Dr. Thompson is dedicated to empowering women-owned businesses and fostering genuine client relationships. She is also a devoted wife, mother, and active participant in her community, constantly striving to uplift and inspire others.

beyondsolutions.biz

PACK HUMOR AND PERSEVERANCE FOR A PIONEERING JOURNEY

Dr. Deb Walters

In 1959, two girls were born. One was a plastic doll named Barbie, meticulously crafted by Mattel, her perfect proportions and long blonde hair setting an unattainable standard of beauty for countless American girls. The other was me, an ordinary girl who embraced life with an optimistic outlook, a strong work ethic, and a pleasant demeanor.

Growing up in a military family, we were constantly moving. By the time I was twelve, I had lived in multiple countries and three states, changing schools five times in two of my grades alone. Being the new, quiet girl was challenging, especially when trying to find my place among established groups. I've always been content with who I am—striving not to *be* the best but to *do* my best. I found something to appreciate in everyone I met, but I never felt the need to conform for popularity or acceptance.

However, my first lesson in peer fashion pressure came in 1977. My mother, a firm believer in frugality, preferred to buy twelve-dollar Lee jeans from the Navy Exchange. I, on the other hand, yearned for a pair of Calvin Klein jeans, which cost sixty-five dollars at the mall. My father, a man of few words, quipped, "When Calvin Klein pays to wear my name across his butt, I'll pay that ridiculous price for his jeans. The jeans your mother buys are just fine for you." His words both offended and struck a chord in me.

Neither Barbie nor Brooke Shields, who modeled those Calvin Klein Jeans, had a significant influence on my self-image. Instead, my experiences growing up in various environments shaped me. I observed the spiritual and emotional struggles people faced on Navy bases during the Vietnam era, the dynamics of Baptist churches, the contrast between Southern culture in America and the cultures of other countries I lived in, and the stories of my grandparents' rural farming roots. These observations became my superpower, providing a solid foundation for my calling into ministry in 1979.

Reflecting on my first two decades of life, I would encapsulate it with the mantra, "What the hell, people! Grow up already and do the next best right thing by God-Self-and-Others."

Answering the call to serve God and others in ministry is not a task for the fainthearted, particularly for a woman. I spent months strolling along the white sands of Pensacola Beach, wrestling with why I shouldn't become a pastoral care minister. I voiced my aspirations to explore the world, capture its beauty through photography, and narrate the resilient and inspiring lives of people. I pleaded these desires to the vast horizon of the Gulf of Mexico, where God paints the sky with daily sunrises and sunsets.

When the internal pull toward spiritual service became too strong to ignore, I spoke to the senior pastor of my home church. He bluntly told me that I had misunderstood my calling—I could marry a minister, but I could never become one. After a lengthy discussion about Baptist politics and influential figures, I retreated to the beach for another heart-to-heart with God.

I am introverted, reserved, and quiet. However, in the face of injustice and disrespect, I channel the fierceness captured in Shakespeare's quote, "Though she be but little, she is fierce." When the church denied me an endorsement letter for seminary, I enrolled at Florida State University instead. The counseling track in the social work department provided me with an experience that far surpassed the seminary's pastoral care curriculum. I was thankful for this superior education, a testament to God's unique sense of humor. I also had to confront my anger toward the sexism prevalent in both family and faith life.

As a social worker, I was tasked with removing a child from their home, and on two occasions, I faced a gun threat. I had to use diplomacy and reason to defuse the situation and leave safely.

In the solitude of my car, I vented my frustrations to God. I spoke of female missionaries in perilous locations, military chaplains in the trenches of war, and social workers navigating volatile domestic situations without police backup. Yet, the church deemed it too risky to allow women to serve as pastoral care and counseling ministers. The irony was not lost on me.

I became the youngest therapist ever hired by the Navy in Florida. I served in a program that evaluated and counseled pilots and service personnel following drug/alcohol offenses. Other career efforts using my skills included running my own decorating business and establishing multiple care/counseling programs in the church, without formal seminary training. Alongside these endeavors, I raised three children with my supportive husband, who never doubted my calling.

Finally, at the age of forty-two, I entered seminary. Dr. William Self, a renowned figure in Baptist life who advocated for women's ministry, was our pastor in 1997. He wrote my endorsement letter for seminary in 2001, ordained me in 2006, and by 2016, I had completed a doctorate in ministry, specializing in spiritual care in loss and lament of soul wounds and compounded grief.

In 1979, female ministers were rare. Today, women still only constitute 19 percent of the ministry. It hasn't been about a battle of the sexes, but about personal growth. I am not bitter, but better for this journey. My mantra today is, "Healthier faith for healthier families for a healthier future worth living out."

For two decades, I've walked a path of service, ministering to those at the end of their life's journey and offering counsel and spiritual care to those still navigating their paths. I've borne witness to stories that weigh heavy on souls. Some narratives are so profound that they seem unfathomable without a higher power, like God, to hold the enormity of the suffering they contain. It is an honor to be a minister of healing and support to such individuals.

During my doctoral studies, a new niche came my way: caring for other ministers. Since 2014, about half of the souls I've served have been fellow ministers, supporting them in their work and personal healing stories.

In 1979, in a Baptist pastor's office, I felt a divine plan unfolding. God had a way around the naysayers and the limited thinkers that seemed to hinder or undermine me. I chose to press on, to grow, and to live a life worth living with God, Self, and Others.

What if we all embarked on life's journey armed with self-awareness, joy, humor, gratitude, perseverance, wisdom, truth, and freedom? These internal companions can enrich our journey, especially if it's a pioneering one. Are you ready to blaze a new trail?

As a new pioneer, you may need some unique tools and awareness to understand what your own call might entail:

- Plan your journey by seeking guidance from wise counsel or a mentor. There will always be challenges to face and obstacles to address. Put in place a determination to remain courageous without false bravado or fear. Get the education and certification needed to be excellent in your implementation of the work you're called to provide. Embrace the transformation process a journey will bring by being resilient without becoming jaded or angry. Grow into the wiser version of yourself by being humble and internally content with yourself.

- Surround yourself with a trusted inner circle. If you are the smartest one in that circle, then your circle is too small. You will always need to have a wiser, strategic and sound-minded voice in the circle to keep you sharp and challenged for the next chapter of the journey.

- Take ownership of your personal choices and your narrative. Every decision you make is an exercise in your use of power, responsibility, and self-control for the trajectory of your own life. Be intentional, present, and authentic to what success and failure teaches you about you. Utilize self-care and reflective spiritual mindfulness practices to direct your life, and various relationships.

- Find your own voice. Discover a personal mantra that resonates with your inner self—a unique phrase, a sacred Scripture, a memorable movie line, or a lyric from a song. Frequently recite it to yourself, especially during moments of deep breathing and perseverance, as a reminder of your true essence when it's time to excel in your endeavors.

- Finally, be prepared to impart the earned wisdom you've gained, the resilience you've developed, and the inspiring tales you've lived. Remember, graveyards are filled with individuals who departed with their unique talents and stories untold. Choose to be someone who enriches others' lives by sharing your life's gifts before your time comes.

When it's my turn to walk into the afterlife, I want to dance into the unknown realm of heaven with gratitude and respect for every good and not-so-good aspect of my life. All of it has informed, transformed, and allowed me to be a wounded healer who offers healing to others.

As Mother Teresa's Anyway Prayer says beautifully, "Give the world the best you have, and it may never be enough; give the world the best you've got anyway. You see, in the final analysis, it is between you and God; it was never between you and them anyway."

Dr. Deb Walters is a professional grief expert who works in spiritual care and grief support. She is director of the Milledgeville Christian Counseling Center in Georgia. A corporate chaplain and psych-social support trainer, Deb holds degrees in social work, seminary training, and a doctorate in grief impacts on the human spirit. She attended Florida State University, and Mercer University McAfee School of Theology. Her programs include Grief Compass, Still Living & Moving Forward Retreats, and Training other colleagues on how to utilize the Enneagram in their coaching and counseling of their clients.

drdebministries.com

FROM DISSONANCE TO CONNECTION: A JOURNEY OF SELF-DISCOVERY

Adele Wang

There I was in a roomful of people, sitting on the edge of my seat like everyone else and eager to hear the wisdom of the esteemed spiritual teacher. I don't remember the question I asked him during his talk. All I remember now is the way his face turned red with anger as he looked me right in eyes and shouted, "Adele, wake up!"

I was shocked. Time stopped. I literally felt blasted out of my body. And in the deafening silence and shame that washed over me as everyone craned to stare at me, something snapped inside of me.

It became painfully clear to me that my relentless pursuit of self-improvement was leading me nowhere. I had been running down a path of trying to feel better that was just making me feel worse. I felt an internal "click" inside that said, "I'm done." Despite all the self-help books, psychology sessions, and now intense spiritual practices, I still felt isolated and disconnected. Especially in my relationships.

And in that painful moment, I felt all my beliefs about what I thought it took to create a meaningful life shatter.

Little did I know that this public humiliation would become the catalyst for a profound transformation—one that would lead me out of a life of constant self-improvement to genuine connection. But it did not go the way I expected.

As a former top violinist, I had always had an intense drive for excellence and perfection. It had propelled me through a successful corporate career. But it had also left me feeling off balance and out of tune with myself. From a young age, I had always believed that if I just improved myself, I would become a more likeable and loveable person. I devoured self-help books, attended many workshops, and immersed myself in a spiritual development program.

The real issue was that I didn't know who I was. So I didn't know the first thing about how to be myself. I'm not sure I even understood what that meant exactly, other than it was some version of a better, more improved version of myself with all the negative issues fixed. I think I subconsciously thought that if I could accomplish that noble goal, a more acceptable and lovable version of me was bound to emerge, and life would be good.

This relentless pursuit of self-improvement came at a heavy emotional cost. My relationships suffered as I struggled to connect authentically with others. On the outside, I was sparkly and social. But on the inside, I was constantly on edge, anxious, and hypercritical. I worried all the time about saying the right thing to people. I thought I had to be really knowledgeable or super understanding. I thought that was what successful relationships involved. I was on empathic overdrive, and it was exhausting.

The spiritual program I had thrown myself into was supposed to be different. Here, among like-minded individuals, I thought I would finally find my harmonic resonance. To finally rock and roll with joy and meaning in life.

Instead, I found myself caught in the same cycle of seeking and self-criticism. Only now it had an added layer of spiritual jargon and expectations. The pressure to be "more spiritual" and "more conscious" only added to my growing sense of being out of rhythm with my own life.

When that spiritual teacher shouted at me, I realized that none of the things I had tried had brought me the peace and connection I craved. It was just about doing more "work." It was as if I suddenly realized I had been practicing scales for years for a symphony performance of life that never got started. It felt like a cruel joke had been played on me, by myself and life.

After the presentation, I went home and fell into a deep depression. Internally I gave up on myself, since I had tried everything I could think of and nothing had worked. I thought about leaving this life. I withdrew from my spiritual community. Curiously, I discovered I didn't actually miss them like I thought I would. Somehow I stumbled through each day in a dull, muffled, gray state. I did the bare minimum to get through the day and just wanted to be left alone. I don't remember much from this time. It's rather hazy.

Yet, as painful as it was, it was only by going through this state of finally giving up and surrendering that I finally found my way out.

I do think it is sometimes like this in life. At times, change only comes after hitting absolute rock bottom.

Somehow, through a series of odd events, I encountered a woman who would change the course of my life. She introduced me to a completely different way of connecting to life and myself—focused not on thinking on how to be spiritual but instead tuning into the vibrant world of color, sound, and movement within myself.

For the first time in my life, I began to feel a genuine connection—a resonance—with myself.

I began to experience my life in a more embodied, sensual way. I became aware of the internal rhythms of my body and the vital energy of aliveness. I became much more connected with my natural feminine essence. It was like seeing a color I had never noticed before, hearing a song I had never heard played. Instead of trying to think my way to happiness, I was learning to feel my way into being, to dance with the ever-changing cadences of life.

As I delved deeper into this work, I began to understand the fundamental flaws in my previous approaches, and I empathized with others who had struggled as I had. They, like me, were intelligent people who felt isolated, stuck in their minds, and trying so hard to fix themselves so they could find more love. They were successful on the outside but emotionally lost on the inside. And they were completely disconnected from their bodies.

I discovered a key distinction: Being curious and wanting to grow is natural and healthy, but presuming this needs to be done through fixing and improving oneself is not. This was the rabbit hole in which I had gotten caught, and I think a lot of us get caught here too. It's a model that takes us down a road that goes nowhere because it presupposes there is something wrong with us to begin with that needs fixing . . . for our own good. Even less useful is the idea that our minds can fix themselves— that we can "raise consciousness" through correct thinking.

This internal shift was transformative for me. As I worked with this woman, the quality of my relationships with others deepened in unexpected and delightful ways. The anxiety and hyper-empathic overdrive that had plagued me my whole life began to dissolve. I connected to an amazing man, after many years of despairing that I would ever find anyone, and we got married. My business flourished without extra effort. I realized how much of my life I had spent more time thinking about life and relationships instead of allowing myself to fully experience things deeply.

Today, I feel more connected to myself and others than I ever thought possible. If I could do it, I believe anyone can. This experience has equipped me to serve many professionals grappling with the same issues. I believe the pressures of the corporate world and entrepreneurship exacerbate these internal struggles, muffling the vibrant, creative energy that exists within all of us. I understand my clients because I was there. I remember the constant drive to be "on" while being unable to silence the inner critic. I discovered, to my chagrin, that just knowing intellectually what my issues were did not actually change anything. I understood myself better, but I didn't actually feel better.

I believe that embodiment and an intuitive sense of the energy is a thousand times more powerful than focusing on positive thinking. No one really needs to fix or improve themselves. Processing issues is overrated, and we're a culture obsessed with processing. Instead, it's more useful to discover and play your own song instead of someone else's. Find your piece, and you will find your peace.

I hope my story helps inspire you to explore the transformative power of being you. Play your song in the grand symphony of life. Hear the poetry of your unique rhythm, colors, textures, melody, and harmony. When you learn to do this, you find that the symphony of life has been playing all along—you just needed to learn how to listen.

Adele Wang is a premier mentor for stressed professionals who want lives of more purpose and connection. As a spiritual teacher and storyteller, she has helped thousands of clients around the world reduce anxiety and create success at a time where there's been more change and uncertainty than ever. A frequent speaker and host of the *All Things Human* podcast, she also guides business leaders through the human side of AI. She holds an MS in Industrial Relations and a BA in Economics from the University of Wisconsin. She loves dogs, sunsets, and music of all kinds.

adelewang.com

www.ingramcontent.com/pod-product-compliance
Lightning Source LLC
Chambersburg PA
CBHW070126030426
42335CB00016B/2282